# The
# Meaning of Life
*from a Buddhist Perspective*

# The
# Meaning of Life
## from a Buddhist Perspective

Tenzin Gyatso
the Fourteenth Dalai Lama

*Translated and edited by*
*Jeffrey Hopkins*

Wisdom Publications · Boston

Wisdom Publications
361 Newbury Street
Boston, Massachusetts 02115

Text © 1992 Tenzin Gyatso, the Fourteenth Dalai Lama and Jeffrey Hopkins
Line drawings © 1993 Wisdom Publications

Color photographs of the Wheel of Life by Elizabeth Napper and Daniel E. Perdue
from a thangka in the possession of Daniel E. Perdue.

*Library of Congress Cataloging-in-Publication Data*
Bstan-'dzin-rgya-mtsho, Dalai Lama XIV, 1935-
  The meaning of life from a Buddhist perspective /
  Tenzin Gyatso, the Fourteenth Dalai Lama;
  translated and edited by Jeffrey Hopkins.
      p.  cm.
    Translation of a series of lectures in Tibetan given in
  London, 1984.
    Includes bibliographical references and index.
    ISBN 0–86171–096–7 (acid-free paper) :
    1. Buddhism—Doctrines.
    2. Religious life—Buddhism.
  I. Hopkins, Jeffrey. II. Title.
  BQ7935.B774M4 1991
  294.3'42—dc20                                    91–30315

  10  9  8  7  6  5  4  3
  98  97  96  95  94

Set in Sabon by Coghill Composition, Virginia. Printed at Northeast Impressions,
Fairfield, New Jersey, USA.

# Contents

# Foreword

THE Gere Foundation is delighted to sponsor Wisdom's publication of *The Meaning of Life from a Buddhist Perspective* by His Holiness the Dalai Lama.

Winner of the 1989 Nobel Prize for Peace, the Dalai Lama is universally regarded as one of the great spiritual friends of our twentieth century. He is the product of an unbroken lineage extending back to the historical Buddha. His forty years as a spiritual teacher and political leader are unique in our time. A brilliant scholar, his words and experience go far beyond the academic. His teachings are rooted in a life tried and tested, a life dedicated to peace, human rights, social change and the total transformation of the human mind and heart. These can only be achieved through a fearless non-violence guided by both a transcendent wisdom and an unshakable universal altruism. "My religion is kindness," he has often said.

Since the Chinese invasion of independent Tibet in 1950, and his harrowing escape to India in 1959, His Holiness has worked tirelessly to free his people from a brutal and systematic genocide that has left 1,200,000 Tibetans dead (a fifth of the pre-invasion population). The unfaltering patience and compassion he has shown for those who continue to destroy his country are finally beginning to bear fruit, and the restoration of Tibetan independence is within sight. The ability to adhere to, embody and generate Buddhist principals under extreme adversity is the mark of a true Bodhisattva.

This book is a wondrous opportunity for us all to make contact with such a man and his teachings. Readers will derive much benefit from contemplating and meditating on them. The Gere Foundation is proud to be associated with His Holiness and his message of universal responsibility and peace, and pleased to support Wisdom Publications in its efforts to promote these ideals. May this book bring happiness and the causes of future happiness to all beings.

Richard Gere
New York

# Preface

WHY are we in this situation? Where are we going? How should we live our lives? Do our lives have any meaning? In the spring of 1984, His Holiness the Dalai Lama, recipient of the 1989 Nobel Peace Prize, addressed issues such as these from a Buddhist perspective in a series of lectures at Camden Hall, London. In five sessions over three days, he presented the basic world view of Buddhism: how Buddhism views the position of beings in the world and how human beings can make their lives meaningful.

These lectures elaborate on the meaning of life by pointing out the causes behind our situation as well as the altruistic purpose to which life can be put. Addressed primarily to a Buddhist audience, the lectures clarify a view of inner psychic cosmology that has had great influence throughout Asia. From a vivid description of how we become trapped in a counter-productive maelstrom of suffering, there emerges a sense of how Buddhists place themselves in the universe. The unsettling description of the steps of entrapment is in fact a call to action, for it shows how, through reversing the process, the limiting prison of selfishness can be turned into a source of help and happiness for others.

The way in which this process plays itself out in the nitty-gritty of everyday life is shown in the Dalai Lama's answers to a myriad of questions from the audience at the beginning of the second through fifth lectures. He elaborates on technical issues raised during the lectures and considers many of the difficult problems we encounter in our lives: how to deal with aggression from within and without; how to reconcile personal responsibility with the doctrine of selflessness; how to handle a loss of faith in a guru or lama; how to face a terminal illness; how to help someone who is dying; how to reconcile love for family with love for all beings; and how to integrate practice in daily life. The Dalai Lama addresses these and other issues and concerns with heartening directness.

An underlying theme of all five lectures and the focus of the last is the fundamental innate mind of clear light. The Dalai Lama describes the obscuration of this basically pure and innermost mind and its manifestation in the wisdom realizing the emptiness of inherent existence through implementation of tantric techniques. Indeed, the mind of clear light radiates through his entire presentation of the harrowing process of cyclic existence, in which ignorance of the basic nature of phenomena leads beings into actions that leave potencies in the mind which ripen into more suffering. The mind of clear light is the backdrop against which the process can be addressed in great detail.

The Dalai Lama's intelligence, wit, and kindness suffuse the lectures. His emphasis on peaceful solutions to personal, familial, national, and international problems mitigates against making allegiance to a particular system a goal of life. He makes it clear that theoretical systems should be used to serve beings, and not the other way around. He calls on his listeners to use ideology for the sake of betterment and improvement.

I served as the interpreter for these lectures and have re-translated them for this book in an attempt to capture the detail and nuance often missed under the pressure of immediate translation. I wish to thank Geshe Yeshi Thabkhe of the Central Institute of Higher Tibetan Studies in Sarnath, India, and Joshua Cutler of the Tibetan Buddhist Learning Center in Washington, New Jersey, for help with the stanzas cited in the first lecture. I also wish to express my gratitude to Steven Weinberger and David Need for reading the entire manuscript and making many helpful suggestions.

Jeffrey Hopkins
University of Virginia

# Technical Note

THE names of Tibetan authors and orders are given in "essay phonetics" for the sake of easy pronunciation; for a discussion of the system used, see the Technical Note at the beginning of my *Meditation on Emptiness* (London: Wisdom Publications, 1983), pp.19–22. Transliteration of Tibetan in parentheses and in the glossary is done in accordance with a system devised by Turrell V. Wylie; see "A Standard System of Tibetan Transcription", *Harvard Journal of Asiatic Studies*, vol. 22, 1959, pp.261–7. For the names of Indian scholars and systems used in the body of the text, *ch*, *sh*, and *ṣh* are used instead of the more usual *c*, *ś*, and *ṣ* for the sake of easy pronunciation by non-specialists.

A list of technical terms in English, Sanskrit, and Tibetan is provided in the Glossary at the end of the book.

The
Meaning of Life
*from a Buddhist Perspective*

# 1   *The Buddhist World View*

Tuesday Morning

FIRST, let me talk to the Buddhist practitioners in the audience about the proper motivation for listening to lectures on religion. A good motivation is important. The reason why we are discussing these matters is certainly not for money, fame, or any other aspect of our livelihood during this life. There are plenty of activities that can bring these. The main reason why we have come to Camden Hall stems from a long-term concern.

It is a fact that everybody wants happiness and does not want suffering; there is no argument about this. But there is disagreement about how to achieve happiness and how to overcome problems. There are many types of happiness and many ways to achieve them, and there are also a great variety of sufferings and ways to overcome them. As Buddhists, however, we aim not merely for temporary relief and temporary benefit but for long-term results. Buddhists are concerned not only for this life but for life after life, on and on. We count not weeks or months or even years, but lives and eons.

Money has its uses, but it is limited. Among worldly powers and possessions, there are, doubtless, good things, but they are limited. However, from a Buddhist viewpoint, mental development will go from life to life, because the nature of mind is such that if certain mental qualities are developed on a sound basis, they always remain and, not only that, can increase. In fact, once properly developed, good qualities of mind eventually increase infinitely. Therefore spiritual practice brings both happiness in the long-term and more inner strength day by day.

So keep your mind on the topics being discussed; listen with a pure motivation—without sleep! From my side also, the main motivation is a sincere feeling for others, concern for others' welfare.

## BEHAVIOR AND VIEW

Meditation is needed in developing mental qualities. The mind is definitely something that can be transformed, and meditation is a means to transform it. Meditation is the activity of familiarizing your mind, making it acquainted, with a new meaning. Basically, it means getting used to the object on which you are meditating.

Meditation is of two types—analytical and stabilizing. First, an object is analyzed, after which the mind is set one-pointedly on the same object in stabilizing meditation. Within analytical meditation, there are also two types:

1 an object of meditation, such as impermanence, is taken as the object of the mind and one meditates *on* it;

2 a mental attitude is meditatively cultivated, as in cultivating love, in which case the mind becomes of the nature of the object meditated.

To understand the purpose of meditation, it is helpful to make a division of practices into view and behavior. The main factor is behavior, for this is what induces both one's own and others' happiness in the future. In order for behavior to be pure and complete, it is necessary to have a proper view. Behavior must be well-founded in reason, and thus a proper philosophical view is necessary.

What is the main thrust of Buddhist practices concerning behavior? It is to tame one's mental continuum—to become non-violent. In general in Buddhism, the vehicles, or modes of practice, are divided into Great and Lesser. The Great Vehicle is primarily concerned with the altruistic compassion of helping others, and the Lesser Vehicle is primarily concerned with the non-harming of others. Thus, the root of all of the Buddhist teaching is compassion. The excellent doctrine of the Buddha has its root in compassion, and the Buddha who teaches these doctrines is even said to be born from compassion. The chief quality of a Buddha is great compassion, this attitude of nurturing and helping others being the reason why it is suitable to take refuge in a Buddha.

The *sangha,* or virtuous community, are those who, practicing the doctrine properly, assist others to gain refuge. They have four special qualities. The first is that if someone harms them, they do not respond with harm; the second is that if someone displays anger to them, they do not react with anger; the third is that if someone insults them, they do not answer with insult; and the fourth is that if someone accuses them, they do not retaliate. This is the style of behavior of a monk or nun. The root of these again meets back to compassion; thus, the main qualities of the spiritual community also stem from compassion. In this way, the three refuges for a Buddhist—Buddha, doctrine, and spiritual community—all have their root in compassion.

All religions are the same in having powerful systems of good advice with respect to the practice of compassion. The basic behavior of non-violence, motivated by compassion, is needed not only in our daily lives but also nation to nation, throughout the world.

With respect to the Buddhist view, dependent-arising is the general philosophy of all Buddhist systems even though there are many different interpretations of it. In Sanskrit the word for dependent-arising is *pratītyasamutpāda.* The word *pratītya* has three different meanings—meeting, relying, and depending—but all three, in terms of their basic import, mean dependence. *Samutpāda* means arising. Hence, the meaning of *pratītyasamut-pāda* is that which arises in dependence upon conditions, in reliance upon conditions, through the force of conditions. On a subtle level, it is explained as the main reason why phenomena are empty of inherent existence.

In order to reflect on the fact that things—the subjects on which a meditator is reflecting—are empty of inherent existence because of being dependent-arisings, it is necessary to identify the subjects of this reflection, these being the phenomena that produce pleasure and pain, help and harm, and so forth. If one does not understand cause and effect well, it is extremely difficult to realize that these phenomena are empty of inherent existence by reason of the fact that they are dependent-arisings. One has to understand the presentation of cause and effect—that certain causes help and harm in certain ways—because these are the bases with respect to which emptiness is to be realized by reason of their being dependently arisen. Hence, Buddha set forth a presentation of dependent-arising in connection with the cause and effect of actions in the process of life in cyclic existence so that penetrating understanding of the process of cause and effect could be gained.

Thus, there is one level of dependent-arising that is concerned with causality, in this case the twelve branches, or links, of dependent-arising of life in cyclic existence: ignorance, action consciousness, name and form, the six sense spheres, contact, feeling, attachment, grasping, "existence", birth, and aging and death. Then there is a second, deeper level of dependent-arising that applies to all objects; this is the establishment of phenomena dependent upon their parts. There is no phenomenon that does not have parts, and thus every phenomenon is imputed in dependence upon its parts.

There is a third, even deeper level, which is the fact that phenomena are merely imputed by terms and conceptuality in dependence upon their bases of imputation. When objects are sought among their bases of imputation, there is nothing to be found that is the object imputed, and thus phenomena are merely dependently arisen in the sense of being imputed in dependence upon bases of imputation. Whereas the first level of dependent-arising refers to the arising of compounded phenomena in dependence upon causes and conditions and thus applies only to impermanent, caused phenomena, the other two levels apply to both permanent and impermanent phenomena.

When Buddha set forth the twelve links of dependent-arising, he spoke from a vast perspective and with great import. He taught the twelve links in detail in the *Rice Seedling Sūtra*.[1] As in other discourses, the context is one of questions and Buddha's answers. In this Sūtra, Buddha speaks of dependent-arising in three ways:

1 Due to the existence of this, that arises.

2 Due to the production of this, that is produced.

3 It is thus: due to ignorance there is compositional action; due to compositional action there is consciousness; due to consciousness there are name and form; due to name and form there are the six sense spheres; due to the six sense spheres there is contact; due to contact there is feeling; due to feeling there is attachment; due to attachment there is grasping; due to grasping there is the potentialized level of karma called "existence"; due to "existence" there is birth; and due to birth there are aging and death.

When in the first rendition Buddha says, "Due to the existence of this, that arises," he indicates that the phenomena of cyclic existence arise not through the force of supervision by a permanent deity but due to specific conditions. Merely due to the presence of certain causes and conditions, specific effects arise.

In the second phase, when Buddha says, "Due to the production of this, that is produced," he indicates that an unproduced, permanent phenomenon such as the general nature[2] propounded by the Sāṃkhya system cannot perform the function of creating effects. Rather, the phenomena of cyclic existence arise from conditions that are impermanent by nature.

Then the question arises: If the phenomena of cyclic existence are produced from impermanent conditions, could they be produced from just any impermanent factors? This would not be sufficient; thus, in the third phase, he indicates that the phenomena of cyclic existence are not produced from just any imperma-

---

[1] *sā lu'i ljang pa'i mdo, śālistambasūtra*; P876, vol. 34.
[2] *rang bzhin, prakṛti; spyi gtso bo, sāmānyapradhāna*.

nent causes and conditions but rather from specific ones that have the potential to give rise to specific phenomena.

Setting forth the dependent-arising of suffering, Buddha shows that suffering has ignorance—obscuration—as its root cause. This impure, faulty seed produces an activity that deposits in the mind a potency that will generate suffering by producing a new life in cyclic existence. It eventually has as its fruit the last link of dependent-arising, the suffering of aging and death.

With regard to the twelve links of dependent-arising, there are basically two modes of explanation, one in terms of thoroughly afflicted phenomena and another in terms of pure phenomena. Just as in the four noble truths, which are Buddha's root teaching,[3] there are two sets of cause and effect, one set for the afflicted class of phenomena and another for the pure class, so here in the twelve links of dependent-arising, there are procedures in terms of both afflicted phenomena and pure phenomena. From among the four noble truths, true sufferings—the first truth—are effects in the afflicted class of phenomena, and true sources—the second truth—are their causes. In the pure class of phenomena, true cessations, the third truth, are effects in the pure class, and true paths, the fourth truth, are their causes. Similarly, when it is explained in the twelve links of dependent-arising that due to the condition of ignorance, action is *produced* and so forth, the explanation is in terms of the afflicted procedure, and when it is explained that due to the *cessation* of ignorance, action *ceases* and so forth, it is in terms of the procedure of the pure class. The first is the procedure of the production of suffering, and the second is the procedure of the cessation of suffering.

To repeat: the twelve links of dependent-arising are laid out in terms of a process of affliction and in terms of a process of purification, and each of these is presented in forward and reverse orders. Thus, in the forward process, it is explained that:

---

[3] For a series of lectures structured around the four noble truths, see Dalai Lama XIV, *The Dalai Lama at Harvard: Lectures on the Buddhist Path to Peace* (Ithaca: Snow Lion Publications, 1989).

Due to the condition of ignorance, action arises;
due to the condition of action, consciousness arises;
due to the condition of consciousness, name and form
   arise;
due to the condition of name and form, the six sense
   spheres arise;
due to the condition of the six sense spheres, contact
   arises;
due to the condition of contact, feeling arises;
due to the condition of feeling, attachment arises;
due to the condition of attachment, grasping arises;
due to the condition of grasping, the potentialized level
   of karma called "existence" arises;
due to the condition of "existence", birth arises;
due to the condition of birth, aging and death arise.

Because this mode describes how suffering is produced, it is an explanation of the sources[4] that produce suffering.

In reverse order it is explained that:

The unwanted sufferings of aging and death are produced in dependence upon birth;
birth is produced in dependence upon the potentialized
   level of action called "existence";
"existence" is produced in dependence upon grasping;
grasping is produced in dependence upon attachment;
attachment is produced in dependence upon feeling;
feeling is produced in dependence upon contact;
contact is produced in dependence upon the six sense
   spheres;
the six sense spheres are produced in dependence upon
   name and form;
name and form are produced in dependence upon consciousness;
consciousness is produced in dependence upon action;
action is produced in dependence upon ignorance.

---

[4] *kun 'byung, samudaya.*

Here the emphasis is on the first of the four noble truths, true sufferings themselves, which are the effects.

Then, in terms of the process of purification, it is explained that:

> When ignorance ceases, action ceases;
> when action ceases, consciousness ceases;
> when consciousness ceases, name and form cease;
> when name and form cease, the six sense spheres cease;
> when the six sense spheres cease, contact ceases;
> when contact ceases, feeling ceases;
> when feeling ceases, attachment ceases;
> when attachment ceases, grasping ceases;
> when grasping ceases, the potentialized level of karma
>     called "existence" ceases;
> when the potentialized level of karma called "existence"
>     ceases, birth ceases;
> when birth ceases, aging and death cease.

This explanation is in terms of the purified class of phenomena with the emphasis being on the causes, that is to say, true paths, from among the four noble truths.

In reverse order, it is explained that:

> The cessation of aging and death arises in dependence
>     upon the cessation of birth;
> the cessation of birth arises in dependence upon the
>     cessation of the potentialized level of karma called
>     "existence";
> the cessation of the potentialized level of karma called
>     "existence" arises in dependence upon the cessation
>     of grasping;
> the cessation of grasping arises in dependence upon the
>     cessation of attachment;
> the cessation of attachment arises in dependence upon
>     the cessation of feeling;
> the cessation of feeling arises in dependence upon the
>     cessation of contact;

the cessation of contact arises in dependence upon the
   cessation of the six sense spheres;
the cessation of the six sense spheres arises in dependence upon the cessation of name and form;
the cessation of name and form arises in dependence
   upon the cessation of consciousness;
the cessation of consciousness arises in dependence
   upon the cessation of action;
the cessation of action arises in dependence upon the
   cessation of ignorance.

Here, within the process of purification the emphasis is on the
effects, true cessations, the third of the four noble truths.

These processes are depicted in a painting called the wheel of
cyclic existence with five sectors[5] [see Pls. 1–7]. Within cyclic
existence, the levels of gods and demi-gods are combined in one
sector, and then there is a sector of humans, these comprising the
happy transmigrations, depicted in the top half of the wheel. The
three sectors in the bottom half are bad or low transmigrations—
those of animals, hungry ghosts, and hell-beings. All of these
sectors represent the levels of suffering in terms of types of birth.

Due to what conditions do these forms of suffering arise? The
circle just inside the five sectors of beings indicates that these
levels of suffering are produced by karma—by actions. It is in
two halves. The half on the right, which has a white base with
people looking and moving upward, symbolizes virtuous actions,
these being of two types, meritorious and unfluctuating; such
actions are the means of attaining lives as humans, demi-gods,
and gods. The left half, which has a dark base with people facing
downward, symbolizes non-virtuous actions, which impel lifetimes in the lower realms.

From what do these karmas that are sources of suffering arise?
They stem from a further source of suffering—the afflictive
emotions of desire, hatred and ignorance—indicated by the innermost circle where a pig, a snake, and a rooster are drawn. The

---

[5] *srid pa'i 'khor lo cha lnga pa.* The one pictured here has six sectors, with separate
sectors for gods and demi-gods.

pig symbolizes ignorance; the snake, hatred; and the rooster, desire. In some versions of the painting, the tails of the rooster and the snake are grasped by the mouth of the pig, thereby indicating that desire and hatred have ignorance as their root. Also, the tail of the pig is grasped in their mouths to indicate that each of them acts to assist and further the other.

The symbolism of these three circles, moving from the center outwards, is that the three afflictive emotions of desire, hatred, and ignorance give rise to virtuous and non-virtuous actions, which, in turn, give rise to the various levels of suffering in cyclic existence. The outer rim symbolizing the twelve links of dependent-arising indicates *how* the sources of suffering—actions and afflictive emotions—produce lives within cyclic existence. The fierce being holding the wheel symbolizes impermanence. If I may make a joke, it does not symbolize a creator-deity! The essential point is to symbolize impermanence; this is why the being is a wrathful monster, though there is no need for it to be drawn with ornaments and so forth as it is here. Once I had such a painting drawn with a skeleton rather than a monster, in order more clearly to symbolize impermanence.

The moon on the far right side indicates liberation. The Buddha on the left is pointing to the moon, indicating that the liberation that causes one to cross the ocean of suffering of cyclic existence should be actualized.

With regard to the history of this painting, at the time of Shākyamuni Buddha, an outlying king, Udayana, made a present of a jewelled robe to the king of Magadha, Bimbisāra, who did not have anything of equivalent worth to give in return. Bimbisāra was worried about this and asked Buddha what he should give. Buddha indicated that he should have a wheel of cyclic existence with five sectors drawn and have the following stanzas put with it:

> Undertaking this and leaving that,
> Enter into the teaching of the Buddha.
> Like an elephant in a thatch house,
> Destroy the forces of the Lord of Death.

Those who with thorough conscientiousness
Practice this disciplinary doctrine
Will forsake the wheel of birth,
Bringing suffering to an end.

Buddha told Bimbisāra to send this to King Udayana. It is said that when the king received the picture and studied it, he attained realization.[6]

The twelve links of dependent-arising are symbolized by the twelve pictures around the outside. The first, at the top—an old person, blind and hobbling with a cane—symbolizes ignorance, the first link. In this context, ignorance is obscuration with respect to the actual mode of being of phenomena. Since within the Buddhist philosophical schools there are four main systems of tenets and, within those schools, there are many different divisions, there are many interpretations of what ignorance is. Not only do we not have time to discuss all of these, I do not even remember all of them!

In general, with respect to ignorance, there is a factor that is a mere non-knowing of how things actually exist, a factor of mere obscuration. Also, in Sūtra, nineteen different types of ignorance are described—various types of wrong views related with extreme positions. However, here in the twelve links of dependent-arising, ignorance is explained to be a wrong consciousness that conceives the opposite of how things actually do exist.

Ignorance is the chief of the afflictive emotions that we are seeking to abandon, each of which is of two types, innate and intellectually acquired. Intellectually acquired afflictive emotions are based on inadequate systems of tenets, such that the mind imputes or fosters new afflictive emotions through conceptuality. These are not afflictive emotions that all sentient beings have and cannot be the ones that are at the root of the ruination of beings—

---

[6] For more about this story, see Sermey Geshe Lobsang Tharchin, *King Udrayana and the Wheel of Life* (Howell, New Jersey: Mahayana Sutra and Tantra Press, 1984), pp. 7–19.

*First link :* IGNORANCE

the latter are *innate*. As Nāgārjuna says in his *Seventy Stanzas on Emptiness*:[7]

> That consciousness conceiving things—which are produced
> In dependence upon causes and conditions—to ultimately exist
> Was said by the Teacher to be ignorance.
> From it the twelve links arise.

---

[7] *stong pa nyid bdun cu pa'i tshig le'ur byas pa, śūnyatāsaptatikārikā*; P5227, vol.95; Toh 3827, Tokyo *sde dge* vol.1. See the Bibliography for editions and translations.

Thus, this is a consciousness that innately misapprehends, or misconceives, phenomena as existing under their own power, as not dependent.

From the fact that this consciousness has different types of objects, ignorance is divided into one type that conceives inherent existence within observing persons and another type that conceives inherent existence within observing other phenomena. These are called consciousnesses conceiving, respectively, a self of persons and a self of phenomena.

The conception of a self of persons is of two types; one is to take cognizance of another person and to consider that person to be inherently existent, and the other is to take cognizance of one's own person, one's own I, and to consider oneself to be inherently existent. The latter is called the false view of the transitory collection.[8] In the stanza cited just above, Nāgārjuna indicates that the innate false view of the transitory collection, which is the root of cyclic existence, is the conception of one's own self as inherently existent and that it arises in dependence upon the conception of those mental and physical aggregates that are the bases of designation of oneself—one's mind, body and so forth—as inherently existent. In this way, the conception of a self of phenomena acts as a basis for the innate false view of the transitory collection that is a conception of the person as inherently existent, even though both are ignorant consciousnesses that conceive inherent existence. Also, there is another, coarser type of innate conception of a self of persons in which persons are misapprehended as being substantially existent in the sense of being self-sufficient.

When we reflect on our own desire and hatred, we see that they are generated within a conception of oneself as very solid, due to which there comes to be a strong distinction between oneself and others, and consequently attachment for one's own side and hatred for others. Attitudes of desire and hatred have an exaggerated thought of I as their basis, do they not?

There is indeed a conventionally posited, valid I—a self that is

---

[8] *'jig tshogs la lta ba, satkāyadṛṣṭi.*

the doer of actions, that is the accumulator of karma, and that is the person undergoing suffering and so forth as the fruits of those actions. However, when we examine the mode of apprehension of the mind when the I gets to the level of being a trouble-maker, we find that we are conceiving a self-instituting I that is an exaggeration beyond what actually exists. When this I appears to the mind, it does not appear to be designated in dependence upon the aggregates of mind and body; rather, it seems almost as if it has its own separate entity. If it did exist the way it appears in such a solid, independent way, then when one investigated it with the Middle Way reasoning, it definitely should become clearer and clearer. However, when, using the Middle Way reasoning, we search for such an I, it obviously becomes less and less clear until it cannot be found. If it were so concrete and independent, it would be findable under analysis, but the fact that, when we search for it, it cannot be found indicates that, except for just being designated in dependence upon the coming together of certain circumstances, it does not exist. Still, it appears to our minds as if it is something that is concretely pointoutable, something very concrete, and when we assent to this false appearance, we get into trouble.

The conflict between the way the I appears as if it were very concrete and the fact that, when analyzed, it cannot be found indicates that there is a discrepancy between its appearance and how it actually exists. Physicists make a similar distinction between what appears and what actually exists.

In our own experience, we can identify types or levels of desire. When we just see a certain article in a store and have desire for it, that constitutes an initial type of desire, but after we buy it and feel, "This is mine," this is a different level. They are similar in both being attitudes of desire, but they differ in strength.

It is important to distinguish between three levels of appearance and apprehension. In the first level, the object is merely appearing; this is before generating desire, when mere appearance and mere recognition of the object occur. Then, when we feel, "Oh, this is really good," and desire has been generated, there is another level of appearance and apprehension of the object. Again, after having decided to buy the article and having made it our own, cherishing it as our own, there is a third level of appearance and apprehension.

On the first level, even with the mere appearance of the object, it does seem to exist from its own side, to exist inherently; however, the mind is not strongly involved with the object. On the second level, desire for the object is induced by ignorance that apprehends it as existing from its own side. There is a subtle level of desire that can exist at the same time as this consciousness conceiving the object to inherently exist, but when desire becomes stronger, the conception of inherent existence acts as its cause, inducing desire, but does not exist at exactly the same time as desire. It is crucial to identify in your own experience that:

- On the first level there is the appearance of the object as inherently existent.

- On the second level there is a consciousness that assents to this appearance—apprehending the object as inherently existent and thus giving rise to desire.

- On the third level, when we have bought such an inherently pleasant object and made it our own, it becomes involved with a strong conception of ownership in which we consider it to be excessively valuable.

At the end of this process, two very powerful streams of adherence—attachment for the inherently pleasant object and attachment for oneself—have come together, making the desire even greater than before. Reflect on whether or not this is so.

The same is true for hatred. There is an initial level that is conventionally valid perception of the qualities of an object—for instance, seeing something bad and identifying it as bad. However, when it gets to the level of producing hatred upon thinking, "Oh, this is really bad," this is a second level. Then, when it is related with yourself, it is stronger, and when it is seen as potentially bringing harm to yourself, even stronger hatred develops.

Thus, for both desire and hatred, the ignorance that is the conception of inherent existence acts as an assister. In this way, the cause of all this trouble is the pig! And in the Tibetan calendar the year of my birth is called the Year of the Pig!

This is the way obscuration—ignorance—serves as the root of the other afflictive emotions. This ignorant consciousness itself is obscured with respect to the mode of being of phenomena, and hence it is symbolized in the painting by a blind person. Also, since ignorance is weak in the sense that it does not have a foundation of valid cognition, the person hobbles with a cane. More properly, ignorance should be depicted at the bottom of the painting, but it is often put at the top.

In dependence upon such ignorance, the second of the twelve links of dependent-arising, action, occurs. It is called *compositional* action because actions serve to compose or bring about pleasurable and painful effects. It is symbolized by a potter. A potter takes clay and forms it into a new article, and similarly an action begins a sequence that leads to new consequences. Also, once the potter spins the wheel,[9] it will keep turning as long as is needed without further striving and exertion; similarly, when an action has been done by a sentient being, it establishes a predisposition in the mind—or as is said in the Consequence School, it produces a state of destructedness of that action—and this predisposition or state of destructedness has the potential to continue without obstruction until it produces its effect. Even though there is no further exertion, the potency to produce its effect remains just like a potter's wheel which, turned once, remains turning without further exertion.

If effects of actions are considered in terms of consequent rebirths in various ways in the Desire, Form, and Formless Realms, there are virtuous actions and non-virtuous actions, and within virtuous actions there are meritorious actions and nonfluctuating actions. In terms of the door, or approach, through which they are done, there are actions of body, speech, and mind. In terms of their own entities, there are actions of intention[10] and intended actions.[11] In terms of whether the effect is definitely to

---

[9] If well constructed, a potter's wheel will keep turning for a long period of time.

[10] *bsam pa'i las.*

[11] *sems pa'i las.*

1  The wheel of cyclic existence in six sectors.

2　In the middle, the sources of suffering ignorance, (pig), desire, (rooster), and hatred (snake) surrounded by the good and bad actions motivated by them.

3　The sectors of gods and demi-gods.

4 The sectors of humans and gods.

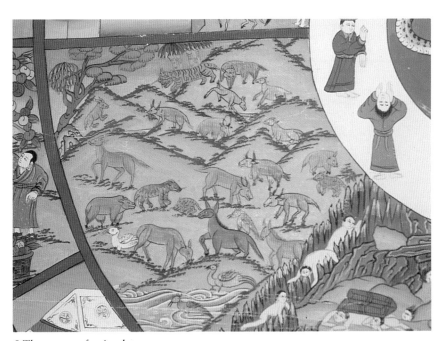

5 The sector of animals.

6 The sector of hungry ghosts.

7 The sector of hell-beings.

*Second link :* COMPOSITIONAL ACTION

be experienced or not, there are definite and indefinite actions. With regard to those actions the effects of which are definitely to be experienced, the effects can be experienced in this lifetime, the next, or a later one.

Also, taking a human lifetime as an example, there are actions that impel or project the general lifetime in a human body, and there are other types of actions that fill in the picture, so to speak. Called completing actions, these fill in the specific qualities—for instance, causing one's body to be beautiful, ugly, and so forth. Consider a human who undergoes many illnesses; as in the case of all other humans, the projecting or impelling karma was a virtuous action as can be determined by the mere fact that the person was born as a human, but the completing actions that fill in the picture by creating a propensity for disease are non-virtuous actions. The opposite occurs when the impelling karma is non-virtuous and the completing actions filling in the picture are virtuous, as in the case of an animal with a good, healthy body. There are also cases in which both the impelling and completing karmas are virtuous, as well as the opposite case in which both are non-virtuous. Thus, there are four types.

Another division of actions is into those done deliberately, those deliberated but not done, those done but not deliberately, and those neither deliberated nor done.[12] Also, there are actions in which (1) the thought is wholesome but the execution of the action is unwholesome, (2) the thought is unwholesome but the execution of it is wholesome, (3) both the thought and the execution are unwholesome, and (4) both the thought and the execution are wholesome. Again, there are karmas whose effects are experienced in common by a number of beings and actions the effects of which are experienced only by one individual.

How are karmas accumulated? For example, during this lecture a particular motivation leads to physical and verbal actions. Good motivation leads to nice words and gentle physical actions, whereby good karma is accumulated. An immediate result is felt in the creation of a peaceful, friendly atmosphere. On the other hand, anger motivates rude words and harsh physical and verbal actions, immediately creating an unpleasant atmosphere. In both cases, with ignorance of the final nature of phenomena as the background, an action is produced; this is the first stage of a karma. Then the action ceases, at which time it imprints a potency, a predisposition, in the consciousness, and the continuum of the consciousness carries this potency to the time of the

---

[12] In lectures at Harvard, the Dalai Lama gave the following examples:

> An example of the first would be to deliberately kill a mosquito. Then, let us suppose that an insect was bothering you, and you wanted very much to kill it, but someone distracts you. In this case, you have karmically accumulated the motivation but you did not carry out the action; this is an action deliberated but not done. An example of an action done but without deliberation would be to kill a mosquito by just moving one's hand without having intended to do so; you killed it, but not deliberately. The fourth type is when one neither has the motivation nor carries out the action.

*The Dalai Lama at Harvard*, p. 60.

*Third link :* CONSCIOUSNESS

fruition of that karma. In this way, an action creates both an immediate result and a potential that eventually brings about either a pleasant or a painful experience in the future.

This is how the first link, ignorance, motivates the second link, action, which establishes a potency for future experience in the third link, consciousness, symbolized by a picture of a monkey. Within Buddhism there is a variety of explanations of the number of consciousnesses; one system asserts only one; others assert six; another asserts eight; and another, nine. Although most Buddhist systems assert six types of consciousnesses, the picture is often one of a monkey going from window to window in a house; it probably has its origins in the assertion of only one consciousness. When this single consciousness perceives by way of the eye, it seems to be an eye-consciousness, and when it perceives by way of the ear, nose, tongue, and body, it seems respectively to be an ear-consciousness, nose-consciousness, tongue-consciousness, and body-consciousness; but it, like the single monkey at many windows, is only one. This is how mind is presented by those who assert only one consciousness. In any case, a monkey is a clever and active animal and thus can symbolize these qualities of consciousness.

A problem is that between an action and its fruition there can be a considerable period of time, yet all Buddhist systems assert that karmas are not lost or wasted; between the cause and the effect there has to be something that connects the two. Many different assertions on what connects an action with its long-range effect are presented within the Buddhist systems. The best solution is offered in the Consequence School, which—pointing out the fact that all systems posit that there is a person at the time of the performance of an action and at the time of experiencing its effect and thus there must be a continuum of a dependently imputed I—holds that the dependently imputed person is the basis of the infusion of the predisposition[13] created by an action. As long as a system is unable to present such a basis of infusion of predispositions, it has to find an independently identifiable basis of infusion of those potencies; this is why the Mind Only School posits a mind-basis-of-all[14] as the basis of infusion of predispositions. However, the highest system, the Consequence School, has no such difficulty since it holds that the continual basis of infusion of predispositions is the mere I, the mere person, and that the temporary basis of infusion of predispositions is the consciousness.

In this way, right after an action, there is a state of destructedness or cessation of that action, which, it could be said, turns into the entity of a predisposition infused in consciousness. The consciousness from this moment right up to just before the moment of conception in the new lifetime is called the consciousness of the causal time or cause-consciousness. The consciousness

---

[13] An action infuses, or deposits, a predisposing potency in the mind when it is about to cease. Both the action and the predisposition that it deposits in the mind are called *karma*.

[14] *kun gzhi rnam par shes pa, ālayavijñāna.*

*Fourth link :* NAME AND FORM

of the very next moment, when connection to the next lifetime is made, is called the effect-consciousness. In terms of its duration, the effect-consciousness lasts from that moment to just before the time of the fourth link, name and form, and thus is extremely brief.

Concerning name and form, "name" refers to the four mental aggregates of feeling, discrimination, compositional factors, and consciousness, and "form" is the aggregate of physical phenomena. In this painting, it is depicted by people riding in a boat; in other pictures, it is symbolized by poles that are leaning against each other. The latter reflects a scriptural teaching of the Mind Only presentation of a mental consciousness, a mind-basis-of-all, and form, which are like the legs of a tripod mutually supporting each other. In the other depiction, the boat symbolizes form, and the people in the boat symbolize the mental aggregates. The period of name and form continues through development of the embryo until it begins to develop the five organs.

# 2 Life Impelled by Ignorance

Tuesday Afternoon

QUESTION AND ANSWER PERIOD

*Question:* Could you please clarify the two types of analytical meditation?

*Answer:* Both analytical meditation and stabilizing meditation are of two types. In the first, you are meditating *on* an object, as is the case when meditating on impermanence; in the other, you are causing your own consciousness to be generated into a state of mind, such as when meditatively cultivating love. When you meditate on impermanence or emptiness, you are taking these as the object of your mind, but when you "meditate" faith or "meditate" compassion, you are not meditating *on* faith or *on* compassion through reflecting on its qualities; rather, you are generating your own consciousness into a faithful or compassionate consciousness.

*Question:* How many types of analytical investigation are there?

*Answer:* Within the Buddhist systems there are four ways of investigating phenomena. The first is to look into the functions that an object performs, such as that fire burns or water moistens; the next is to investigate by way of reasoning based on valid proof; the third is to look into dependence, as in causation; and the last is the reasoning of looking into just the nature of the object, that something is naturally so. I think there are many phenomena that have to be understood in the context of the fourth type of rational inquiry—of its just being the nature of something to be so. It strikes me that this type of reasoning may be used in connection with the topic of karmic causation; for instance, if one harms someone else, then because the *nature* of that action is to bring harm to a sentient being, the result *naturally* is that an effect of harm returns to oneself. Similarly, because helping another sentient being has a *nature* of bringing benefit, the effect that returns to oneself is also beneficial.

Also, if one asks why consciousness has a character of experiencing objects or why physical objects are material, one can indeed look into their respective substantial causes and co-operative conditions, but when one moves the question further and further back, it is probably just that it is the nature of consciousness to be an entity of experience. If one posited a beginning to consciousness, there would be much damage by reasoning to that position; for instance, a luminous and cognitive entity would absurdly be produced by something that is not a luminous and cognitive entity. Since there are many such contradictions in that position, it is better to take the position that there is no beginning to consciousness.

Also, with regard to particles of matter, it is probably the case that consciousness can serve as a co-operative condition of matter in the process of producing it, but the substantial cause of matter must be something material since it must be produced from something of a similar type. For instance, if we consider our own galaxy, or world-system of one billion worlds, in the traditional Buddhist presentation there are eons of vacuity, then eons of formation, then eons of abiding, and then eons of destruction; this series of four phases goes on and on and on, over and over again without end. I wonder whether the substances that produce the particles that are the building blocks during the period of formation are present during the period of the eons of vacuity. Perhaps the particles of space mentioned in the Kālachakra system refer to this. Even if five or six billion years have passed since the big bang, there needs to be an explanation of what prior causal conditions gave rise to it.

From another point of view, there are yogis who cultivate meditative states called the earth-totality, water-totality, and so forth, in which all that appears is just earth or just water, and so forth. The phenomena that are produced through the power of yoga indeed have no limit. For instance, even though we have to posit solidity, things cannot be posited as solid in all respects and in terms of all situations; rather, they are posited as solid only in relation to a particular situation.

*Question:* Please give your definition of I, the self?

*Answer:* Those who do not have any belief in former and future lifetimes perhaps do not pay much attention to what the entity or nature of the self is, but among those who do have such belief there are many different assertions. Many non-Buddhist systems posit a permanent self that goes from lifetime to lifetime. They do this because they see that something goes from one life to another and it is clear that the body does not; they cannot posit something impermanent that goes from life to life, so they posit a permanent, unitary, and independent self that travels from one life to the next.

Within the Buddhist systems, an I is posited, but not in the same way as above. Feeling that the I, or self, must be something that can be posited upon analysis, the lower Buddhist systems hold that something *from within* the impermanent mind and body collection must be posited as the I, or self. Certain of these Buddhist schools posit the mental consciousness; some posit the mind-basis-of-all; some, the continuum of the aggregates; and so forth. However, the supreme of all Buddhist tenet systems, the Consequence School, holds that just as a chariot is imputed in dependence upon its parts and cannot be found among its parts, so a person is just imputed in dependence upon the mental and physical aggregates but cannot be found, under analysis, among any of those aggregates. Thus, not only is the I dependently imputed but all phenomena are dependently imputed; even emptiness is dependently imputed, as is Buddhahood—all appearing and occurring phenomena are just dependently designated.

*Question:* Your Holiness, could you talk about the connection between the five aggregates and the five elements?

*Answer:* First it is necessary to identify the five aggregates; these are forms, feelings, discriminations, compositional factors, and consciousnesses. Within the form aggregate the coarser level is, for instance, our body of flesh, blood, and so forth, and the more subtle levels involve the topic of various winds, or inner energies, described in Highest Yoga Mantra. In Mantra, there are many explanations of connections between the movement of basic physical constituents and inner energies, or winds, in channels whereby different levels of consciousness, conceptual and non-conceptual, are produced.[15]

The remaining four aggregates are called "the bases of the name".[16] These are feeling, discrimination, compositional factors, and consciousness. The aggregate of feelings and the aggregate of discriminations are the mental factors of feeling and discriminations, which are separated out from all the other mental factors[17] into their own separate aggregates. As Vasubandhu says in the *Treasury of Manifest Knowledge,*[18] the reasons for this separate treatment are that discrimination is the source of all dispute and that attachment wanting not to separate from pleasurable feeling and attachment wanting to separate from painful feeling draw one into afflictive actions and hence into cyclic existence. Within the fourth aggregate, compositional factors, there are two main types, compositional factors associated with consciousness and those not associated with consciousness. In general, when we speak about beings with a physical body, they have all five aggregates, but in the Formless Realm there are only the four mental aggregates; however, from the viewpoint of Highest Yoga Tantra, this is only in terms of coarse form.

With respect to the elements, there are the basic four elements which, by name, are called earth, water, fire, and wind. The first

---

[15] For a discussion of levels of mind in connection with the process of dying, see Lati Rinbochay and Jeffrey Hopkins, *Death, Intermediate State, and Rebirth in Tibetan Buddhism* (London: Rider, 1979; rpt. Ithaca: Snow Lion Publications, 1980).

[16] *ming gzhi.*

[17] Feeling and discrimination are two from a standard list of fifty-one mental factors. See *The Dalai Lama at Harvard,* pp. 75–6.

[18] *chos mngon pa'i mdzod, abhidharmakośa*; chapter three. See the Bibliography for editions and translations.

has the name "earth", but the main reference is to solidity and obstructiveness. The meaning of "water" is fluidity and moistening. "Fire" means heat and burning. "Wind" on the coarse level refers even to the air that we breathe in and out, but on a subtler level it refers mainly to types of energies that promote development and change. For instance, in the Kālachakra system it is said that even a dead body still has winds functioning in it, because it continues to undergo change. An additional element is space, which, in reference to the body, means empty cavities and passageways. The Kālachakra system also speaks of particles of space, which are extremely subtle; scientists similarly speak of minute particles in space that serve as a basis for other phenomena.

Those are the five aggregates and the five elements. If you have other questions about these topics, please ask.

*Question:* Since all appearances and all life are just illusion, is it not inconsistent to say that there are levels of appearance, such as those you mentioned this morning?

*Answer:* It is not that life *is* an illusion; rather, it is *like* an illusion. Therefore, we can speak of many different types of discrepancy between the way things appear and the way they actually exist. For instance, something that is actually impermanent can appear to be permanent; also, sometimes things that are actually sources of pain appear to be sources of pleasure. These are types of conflict between the way things actually are and the way they appear. Also, in relation to the final reality, objects appear to exist inherently but actually lack such inherent existence; this is another level of discrepancy between appearance and fact.

*Question:* How does belief or disbelief relate to ignorance?

*Answer:* Mostly we have belief that objects inherently exist; they appear to exist from their own side, and we believe that they exist this way. This type of belief is induced by ignorance.

*Question:* When is desire cause and when is desire effect?

*Answer:* Desire can serve as a cause of later moments of desire; thus, it is a cause, and those later moments of desire are instances of desire that are effects of the previous cause. Since that in relation to which it is considered a cause and that in relation to which it is considered an effect are different, there is no problem.

*Question:* If a predisposition toward an action has formed in one's mind, must one inevitably complete it or is there a way out?

*Answer:* If you are able to bring about a condition that is more powerful than the complementary condition that would cause that karma to manifest, it can be overwhelmed. For instance, through disclosure of ill-deeds, developing contrition, and engaging in virtuous activity aimed at purifying a bad karma, you can purify it. At minimum, you can diminish its force such that, even if you meet with a condition that would have caused it to become activated, it will not.

Let us continue the description of the twelve links of dependent-arising.

## CONDITIONS FOR SUFFERING

THE fifth link is the six sense spheres—the inner promoters of consciousness, which are the eye, ear, nose, tongue, body, and mental senses. In the painting, they are depicted by an empty house because, in terms of birth from a womb, this is a time when the organs are developing but not yet functioning. Thus, like an empty house, the externals required for functioning sense consciousnesses are developing, but internally, in a general sense, they are not yet functioning.

After this, there comes contact, the sixth link. "Contact" itself is a mental factor that distinguishes objects as pleasurable, painful, or neutral upon the coming together of object, sense power, and consciousness. The objects are visible forms, sounds, odors, tastes, tangible objects, and other phenomena not included in those five; the sense powers are the six organs—eye, ear, nose, tongue, body, and mental sense powers. When an object, a sense

*Fifth link* : THE SIX SENSE SPHERES

power, and a former moment of consciousness that can act as an immediately preceding condition are present, a consciousness is generated. As a mental factor, contact distinguishes the object as pleasurable, painful, or neutral.

In general, a consciousness is produced by way of having three conditions. The first is called the observed-object-condition,[19] the object that causes the consciousness to be generated into having its aspect. The second is the dominant condition,[20] which is a sense power that causes a particular consciousness to be able to apprehend only its respective type of object and not another, as when the eye sense power gives a consciousness the capacity to apprehend visual objects and not sounds, for instance. The fact that a consciousness is produced as an experiential entity is due to an immediately preceding consciousness; this is the third type

---

[19] *dmigs rkyen, ālambanapratyāya.*
[20] *bdag rkyen, adhipatipratyāya.*

of condition, called the immediately preceding condition.[21]

Because there is a *meeting* with an object and a distinguishing of it, contact is symbolized by a kiss. "Contact" refers to that period in which the meeting of object, sense power, and consciousness occurs, causing one to distinguish the object as pleasurable, painful, or neutral; it is prior to the production of feeling.

The seventh link of dependent-arising, feeling, is posited as a mental factor that experiences pleasure, pain, or neutral feeling upon the object's having been distinguished as pleasurable, painful, or neutral by contact. According to one system of interpretation, the boundaries of this seventh link range from the initial experience of pleasure and pain through to experiencing the pleasure of orgasm. The picture depicting feeling is that of an eye pierced by an arrow. The eye is such that even a very small condition will cause a great deal of feeling, and in the same way, no matter what kind of feeling we have, pleasurable or painful, we cannot stay still with it—it is very effective, it drives us.

---

[21] *de ma thag rkyen, anantaryapratyāya.*

*Sixth link :* CONTACT

*Seventh link :* FEELING

Pleasurable feeling generates a strong drive for more, and pain generates a strong drive to avoidance.

The eighth and ninth links, attachment and grasping, are both types of desire. The difference between them is that attachment is a phase of desire that is weaker in force, whereas grasping is stronger. There are various divisions of attachment; for instance, desirous attachment is associated with the Desire Realm; attachment to destruction is a wish to be separated from painful feeling; and attachment to the Form and Formless Realms is called attachment to mundane existence.

The picture depicting attachment is that of a person drinking beer. This is easy to understand, is it not? No matter how much you drink beer, even though it makes you fat and you do not want to be fat, you still keep drinking and drinking and drinking it. Attachment is a mental factor that increases desire, without any satisfaction. The boundaries of its occurrence as the eighth link of dependent-arising are from the time of the fourth link, name and form, up to the ninth link, grasping.

Grasping, which means mentally grabbing at an object that one desires, is depicted by a monkey taking fruit. There are four varieties of grasping—at desired objects, at views of self, at bad systems of ethics and conduct, and at any of the remaining types of bad views. Such forms of grasping can be described in terms of both ordinary householders and those who have left the householder life and, though celibate, have an erroneous view. There are, however, more types of grasping than the four described here. For instance, a person who (1) has become temporarily free from desire with respect to the Desire Realm and (2) has a correct view, but (3) seeks to be reborn in a Form or Formless Realm has to accumulate a karma that will impel rebirth in that realm and

*Eighth link :* ATTACHMENT

*Ninth link :* GRASPING

hence will have to have grasping for that type of life. Since such examples are not included in these four types, they are not exhaustive. The list, therefore, is said to be formulated only in order to overcome wrong ideas, not be exhaustive.

In dependence upon name and form, sense spheres, contact, and feeling, one generates attachment to remaining with a pleasurable object and attachment seeking separation from a painful object. When such attachment is produced over and over again in stronger form, this constitutes grasping at desired sense-objects, such as pleasant forms, pleasant sounds, pleasant odors, pleasant tastes, and pleasant tangible objects. Such attachment and grasping serve to further potentialize or charge up the karmic potency—established earlier in the consciousness by an action motivated by ignorance—such that it will cause the attainment of a new life-system in the Desire Realm. When that karma, the

*Tenth link :* EXISTENCE

predisposition established in the mind, is nourished by attachment and grasping such that it has full capacity to produce the next lifetime, it is called "existence", the tenth link. This is a case of giving the name of the effect, a new *existence* in the cyclic round of suffering, to the cause, the fully potentialized karma. In the Consequence School, it is, most likely, a fully potentialized state of the destructedness of an action, which itself is a functioning thing that will produce the next lifetime.

The picture in this tenth link is of a pregnant woman. Just as at this point the karma that will produce the next lifetime is fully potentialized and, though not yet manifest, is ready to produce it, so a woman late in pregnancy has a fully developed child inside the womb that has not yet emerged. The tenth link lasts from the time of the fully potentialized karma up to the beginning of the next lifetime. Within it there are two divisions by time—

one level called "directional"[22] since it is directed toward going to the next lifetime and occurs in the earlier lifetime and another level called "in process"[23] since it refers to the potentialized karma at the time of the intermediate state between the two lifetimes.

The eleventh link is the dependent-arising of birth, depicted by a woman giving birth. The child in the womb of the pregnant woman in the previous picture is now changing state.

The twelfth link is the dependent-arising of aging and death. There are two types of aging; the first is called "progressive" since from the moment of conception one is proceeding in the direction of aging; hence, it occurs in every moment for the rest of the life. The other type is called "deterioration", which is the usual degeneration of old age.

---

[22] *zhol ba.*
[23] *zhugs pa.*

*Eleventh link :* BIRTH

After aging comes death. In between these, there are cries of sorrow and many types of suffering, such as seeking but not getting what you want, getting what you do not want, and so forth.

*Twelfth link :* AGING AND DYING

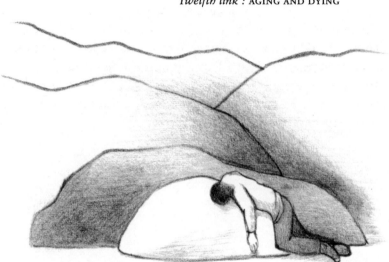

## IGNORANCE AS THE ROOT OF SUFFERING

Our lives begin with the suffering of birth and end with the suffering of death; between these two, there are many different consequences of aging and many unfortunate events. This is suffering, the first of the four noble truths, which we do not want—the problem we want to overcome. It is important to investigate whether there is any way to surmount such suffering or not. To understand this, it is necessary to investigate what the causes of our situation are. This is the relevance of the entire explanation of the twelve links of dependent-arising beginning with the stage of ignorance.

When we examine any type of suffering now being experienced, we find that its root is ignorance. As long as we have ignorance, which is the seed and source of suffering, in any and every minute we can initiate an action that will serve as a cause for another rebirth. Through this process, in our one stream of consciousness we have already deposited limitless predispositions that are potencies established by actions motivated by ignorance; we have a limitless number of such potentialities for future lifetimes in our consciousness right now.

We have been considering the twelve links of dependent-arising in terms of one round—first, ignorance and then the remaining eleven links coming from that. In this context, we can see that simultaneously other rounds of dependent-arising are operating since other instances of ignorance are inducing additional sets. Also, in this explanation in which the twelve are viewed serially with the earlier links leading to the later ones, at the time of the operation of this one round of dependent-arising other rounds are operating together with it. You can see this by the fact that with respect to this one round of dependent-arising, although ignorance, action, and consciousness impel the force producing the next lifetime, between consciousness and name and form there must be the eighth, ninth, and tenth links—attachment, grasping, and existence—in order to activate that potency in the consciousness such that it actually can produce the lifetime indicated by number four, name and form. Also, when you consider numbers eight, nine, and ten—attachment, grasping, and existence—the last being the fully potentialized karma leading to birth, at the time of that particular birth another set of name and form, sense spheres, contact, and feeling will be operating. Again, the attachment, grasping, and existence that must come between links three and four must be preceded by their own respective name and form, sense spheres, contact, and feeling—links four, five, six and seven; thus, there is another round of dependent-arising involved in their production. Hence, a single round of dependent-arising necessarily involves other rounds.

Since the first of the twelve links is ignorance and the last is aging and death, it might look as if there were a beginning and an end, but when you realize that in order to bring about the present round of the twelve links of dependent-arising it is necessary to have other rounds operating simultaneously, you understand that since not one but many sets operate together, there is no end unless ignorance is removed. You see that since the root of it all is ignorance, until ignorance is overcome there is nothing that you can really do about getting rid of this process.

In the twelve-linked dependent-arising of a lifetime in a bad transmigration as an animal, hungry ghost, or hell-being, there is the basic ignorance that is obscuration with respect to the mode of being of phenomena and also ignorance that is obscuration with respect to the relation between actions and their effects. This motivating force of ignorance produces a non-virtuous action that deposits a potency in the consciousness that serves as the projecting cause of a life in a bad transmigration. That projecting cause is actualized or charged up by attachment and grasping such that it becomes fully potentialized as "existence". Due to this, the projected effects (effect-consciousness, name and form, sense spheres, contact, and feeling) and actualized effects (birth and aging/death) of suffering in a bad transmigration are produced.

In the twelve-linked dependent-arising of a lifetime of high status within cyclic existence as a human, god, or demi-god, the basic ignorance is the same—obscuration with respect to the mode of being of phenomena—but the action that is motivated by it is a virtuous action, such as abandoning killing or any other action beneficial to others. Such a virtuous action deposits in the cause-consciousness a good potency for rebirth in a lifetime of high status. This projecting cause is actualized or charged up by attachment and grasping such that it becomes fully potentialized as "existence", whereupon it produces the projected and actualized effects of a lifetime in a condition of high status.

Reflection on how others travel in cyclic existence the same way serves as a technique for increasing compassion. Thus, vast methods of meditation are set forth (1) in terms of reflecting on these twelve links of dependent-arising in oneself, whereby a wish to leave cyclic existence is developed, and (2) in terms of reflecting on these twelve links of dependent-arising in others, whereby compassion increases.

That completes our discussion of dependent-arising as the process of developing a lifetime in cyclic existence.

## Dependent-arising as dependent imputation

Another mode of dependent-arising is the establishment of phenomena in dependence upon their parts. Any and all objects have parts. Physical objects have directional parts, and formless phenomena such as consciousness have temporal parts—earlier and later moments that form their continuum. If there were any such thing as a partless particle to serve as the building-block of larger objects, one could not discriminate between, for instance, its left and right sides or front and back, and if you cannot discriminate sides in something, then no matter how many of them you put together you would not have anything more than the size of the original one. It would be impossible for them to amass. However, it is a fact that gross objects are produced through the coming together of many minute particles; thus, no matter how small the particle is, it must have directional parts, and through this logic it is established that there are no physical objects that are partless.

Similarly, with respect to a continuum, if the smallest moments of a continuum did not have earlier and later parts themselves, there would not be any possibility of their coming together to form a continuum. If a moment had no parts such that what was in contact with what precedes it was also equally in contact with what follows it, there would be no way for such partless moments to form a continuum. Similarly, with respect to unchanging phenomena such as uncompounded space, there are parts or factors such as space in the eastern quarter and space in the western quarter or the part associated with this object and the part associated with that object. Thus any object, whether it is impermanent or permanent, changing or unchanging, has parts.

However, when the whole and parts of any particular object— the latter being that in dependence upon which the whole is imputed—appear to our minds, the whole appears to have its own separate entity and the parts appear to be *its* parts. Is this not the case? Though they depend on each other, they seem to have their own entities. They appear to our conceptual thought in this manner, but if they did, in fact, exist this way, you should be able to point your finger at a whole that is separate from its parts.

Thus, you can see that there is a discrepancy between the way whole and parts appear and the way they actually exist in that they seem to have their own separate entities but actually do not. However, this does not mean there are no objects that are wholes because if there were no wholes, you could not speak of something as being a part of anything, for the whole is that in relation to which something is posited as its part. Hence, there are wholes, but their mode of existence is that they are designated in dependence upon their parts—they do not exist in any other way. This applies not just to changing, impermanent phenomena but also to permanent, unchanging phenomena and thus is broader in meaning than the former interpretation of dependent-arising, which is limited to phenomena arisen in dependence upon causes and conditions.

## Analytical Unfindability

Dependent-arising has a profound implication. It connotes that if one is not satisfied with the mere appearance of an object but seeks, through extended analysis, the actual object to which the imputation is affixed, one does not come up with anything among or separate from the bases of imputation of that object that can be said to be the object. Take the self, or I, as an example: the I is the controller, or user, of mind and body, and the mind and body are the objects of use of that I. The I, body, and mind definitely do exist, and it cannot be denied that they perform their respective functions. The I is like an owner, and the body and mind belong to it. Indeed, we say, "Today there is something wrong with my body; therefore, I am tired." Or, "Today my body is fit; so I am very fresh." Such statements are valid, but with respect to one's arm, for instance, nobody says, "This is I," but still when one's arm is painful, we definitely do say, "I am in pain, I am not well." Despite this, it is clear that the

I and the body are different; the body is something that belongs to the I.

Similarly, we speak of "my mind" or "my consciousness", as when we feel, "My memory is so poor; something is wrong." You can even feel to oppose your own consciousness, your own memory; is it not so? We say such things as, "I want to improve the sharpness of my mind, I want to train my mind," in which case the mind is both the trainer and the object trained. When the mind is unruly—not doing what you want it to—oneself is like the teacher or trainer of the mind and the mind is like the unruly student that is going to be trained to do what you want; you will give it some training in order to make it obey. We say and think such things, and they accord with the facts.

In this way, both body and mind are things that belong to the I, and the I is the owner, but, aside from mind and body, there is no separate, independent entity of I. There is every indication that the I exists; yet, under investigation, you cannot find it. For example, the Dalai Lama's I must be within the confines of this area circumscribed by my body; there is no other place it could possibly be found. This is definite; it is for sure. However, if you investigate within this area what the true Dalai Lama, the true Tenzin Gyatso, is, besides this body and mind the I does not have its own substance. Still, the Dalai Lama is a fact, a man, a monk, a Tibetan, someone who can speak, who can drink, who can sleep, who can enjoy; is it not so? This is sufficient to prove that something exists, even though it cannot be found.

This means that among the bases of imputation of the I there is nothing to be found that is an illustration of the I or that is the I. But does this mean the I does not exist? No, it does not mean this; the I definitely does exist, but when it exists and still cannot be found among its bases of imputation that constitute the place where it must exist, one has to say that it is established not under its own power but through the force of other conditions. It cannot be posited any other way.

Among the conditions in dependence upon which the I exists, one of the more important factors is the conceptuality that designates it. Thus it is said that the I and other phenomena exist through the power of conceptuality. In this way, dependent-arising comes to mean not just "arisen in dependence upon causes and conditions" or "imputed in dependence upon a basis of imputation" but also "arisen or imputed in dependence upon a conceptual consciousness that imputes the object".

Thus in the term "dependent-arising", "dependent"[24] means depending, or relying, on other factors. Once the object depends on something else, it is devoid of being under its own power—it is devoid of being independent. Hence, it is empty of an independent nature, of being under its own power. Nevertheless, it does arise in reliance upon conditions. Good and bad, cause and effect, oneself and others—all objects are established in reliance upon other factors—they arise dependently. Due to being dependently arisen, objects are devoid of the extreme of being under their own power. Also, because, in this context of dependence, help and harm arise and exist, objects do *not* not exist—their performance of functions is feasible. In this way, the causes and effects of actions are feasible, as is the I that is the basis of them. When one understands this, one is released from the extreme of non-existence, nihilism.

In this way, existing in dependence upon conceptuality also is a meaning of dependent-arising—the most subtle meaning. Nowadays, physicists are explaining that phenomena do not exist just objectively in and of themselves but exist in terms of, or in the context of, involvement with a perceiver, an observer.

I feel that the topic of the relation between matter and consciousness is a place where Eastern philosophy—particularly Buddhist philosophy—and Western science could meet. I think that this would be a happy marriage, with no divorce! If we work along the lines of a joint effort by Buddhist scholars—not mere scholars but those who also have some experience—and pure, unbiased physicists to investigate, study, and engage in deeper research in the field of the relation between matter and consciousness, by the next century we may find beautiful things that may be helpful. This does not have to be considered the practice of

[24] *rten, pratītya.*

religion but can be done simply for the extension of human knowledge.

Also, those scientists who are working in the field of neurology on the human brain could benefit from Buddhist explanations about consciousness—how it functions, how it changes in terms of levels, and so forth. Some time back, I asked a neurologist how memory functions. He reported that they still had not found a concrete explanation; so, in this field, too, I think that we could work together. Also, some Western medical professionals are showing interest in the curing of certain illnesses through meditation. This also is an interesting topic for a joint project.[25]

Because of Buddhism's emphasis on self-creation, there is no creator-deity, and thus from this viewpoint some people consider it, strictly speaking, not to be a religion. A Western Buddhist scholar told me, "Buddhism is not a religion; it is a kind of science of mind." In this sense, Buddhism does not belong to the category of religion. I consider this to be unfortunate, but in any case it means that Buddhism becomes closer to science. Furthermore, from the pure scientist's viewpoint, Buddhism naturally is considered a type of spiritual path. Again, it is unfortunate that we do not belong to the category of science. Buddhism thereby belongs to neither religion nor pure science, but this situation provides us with an opportunity to make a link, or a bridge, between faith and science. This is why I believe that in the future we will have to work at bringing these two forces more closely together than they are at present.

The majority of people simply neglect religion, but among those who do not, there is on the one side a group who are following faith and experiencing the value of a spiritual path, and on the other side is a group who are deliberately denying any value to religion. As a result, there is constant conflict between these two factions. If, one way or another, we could help bring these two forces closer, it would be worthwhile.

---

[25] For more discussion of many of the points raised here, see *MindScience: An East-West Dialogue* (Boston: Wisdom Publications, 1991).

# 3 Levels of the Path

Wednesday Morning

*Question:* Your Holiness, would you please clarify the difference between actions of intention and intended actions?

*Answer:* With regard to actions, or karma, in general, there are two different systems—one that explains that any sort of karma is necessarily the mental factor of intention, and another that says that there are also physical and verbal karmas. According to the first system, the mental factor of intention itself, at the time when it is initially motivating an action, is called an action of intention, whereas the mental factor of intention at the time of actually engaging in the deed is called an intended action; thus, both are the mental factor of intention. According to the system that posits that there are also physical and verbal actions, actions of intention are explained similarly, but intended actions occur at the point when the action is displayed physically or verbally, and thus intended actions can be either mental, physical, or verbal. The latter is a more preferable system; it is the assertion of the Consequence School.

*Question:* Regarding consciousness, it was said that in the Middle Way School, as opposed to the Mind Only School, the continual basis of a predisposition caused by an action is the mere I, while the temporary basis was said to be consciousness. Can you explain this further? Specifically, how can the everlasting basis of the predisposition be the mere I, which does not exist inherently or everlastingly? Also, how or what is the mechanism that stores the predisposition since it is not the mind-basis-of-all, and how does it travel from one lifetime to the next?

*Answer:* When we speak of the nominally existent I that is a mere name, this does not mean that except for the name, there is no meaning to I, or self, other than just a name. There is a meaning to which the name I refers. However, because the object I does not exist in a self-instituting way under its own power without depending on that name but exists within depending very much on the name, on conceptual imputation, it is said that it is "name only", merely nominally imputed. Thus, in the term "mere I", the word "mere" eliminates that when the I is sought under analysis, it can be found. Not only is the I—which is the basis into which these predispositions are infused—merely nominally imputed, but also predispositions themselves as well as the actions that infuse the predispositions are nominally imputed, as is everything else. That phenomena are merely nominal does not mean that they do not exist at all; rather, it means that, within existing, they do not exist under their own power, by way of their own entity, by way of their own character.

When it is said that the basis of infusion and of carrying the predispositions is "name-only", it might appear to your mind that then it really would not be anything. However, through this explanation you can understand that this is not the case and that there is no such difficulty. With regard to the means connecting a karma with its effect, consider this: In our conventional vocabulary we say, "At an earlier time I did such and such," and it is a fact that the agent of that action is oneself. From the viewpoint that oneself is a continuation of the mere-I that performed the action, we say this, but if we look into the matter, the action has ceased, and the I of the present moment is not the I of the previous moment. Still, innately we have the thought and indeed say, "I did that," and this accords with the fact. One is, therefore, the owner of that action. In this way, there is a connection between the action and oneself, and this is what connects forward to the future effect of that action no matter how much time passes. Since the continuum of the mere-I of the person who performed the action and thereby accumulated the karma keeps going, one is still the I who accumulated that karma, and since the action that was done earlier has to fructify, there is no one else for whom it can fructify except oneself.

The I is designated in dependence upon the mental and physical aggregates, and in terms of the tantric, or mantric, system there are coarse and subtle levels of those mental and physical aggregates. From the viewpoint of Highest Yoga Tantra, the final basis of imputation of the I has to be a subtle aggregate that has been together with oneself since beginningless time; this is a subtle level of consciousness, the continuum of which is beginningless and uninterrupted, eventually reaching fulfillment in Buddhahood. There is no question about whether afflicted minds will go on to Buddhahood—of course they do not. Even the coarser levels of consciousness do not; it is the most subtle level of consciousness that proceeds to Buddhahood. This subtle level has lasted since beginningless time and continues forever. When we die, our coarser levels of consciousness dissolve. On our last day, at the time of our death the final consciousness that manifests is this most subtle mind of clear light; it is this consciousness that makes the connection to the next lifetime. In this way, the subtler aggregates necessarily exist continuously throughout time.

According to the Consequence School, when an action ceases or disintegrates, that disintegration is something that is caused, and thus the state of having disintegrated that occurs after the disintegration is also something that is caused—it is a produced phenomenon. Thus, the action establishes a state of destructedness that itself is an impermanent phenomenon, continuing until the time of the fruition of the karma and producing the fruition.

With regard to the way in which the I appears, there is a general type of I that has existed since beginningless time right through to the present, but with regard to particular I's, there is an I qualified, for instance, by one's own youth, and there is an I qualified by being related with a human lifetime as distinct from another type of life, and so on. For instance, we refer to the I of our own youth, "Oh, I used to be such a rascal when I was young, but nowadays I have improved a bit." Many such distinctions are to be made within the I, one more general and pervasive and others more individual and less pervasive.

*Question:* Is material energy the same as mental energy?

*Answer:* In general, because matter and consciousness are different, it seems that the energy associated with them would be different. With respect to mental energy, there are many grosser and subtler levels of consciousness; the grosser a level of consciousness is, the more it is related with the present body, whereas the subtler a consciousness is, the less connection it has with the gross physical body. Also, the subtler levels of mind are more powerful than the grosser levels, and thus if one is able to utilize them, they are more effective for mental transformation. In order to discuss differences of energy, one has to consider many different levels of matter and consciousness.

*Question:* How can we abandon innate ignorance?

*Answer:* Certain types of ignorance can be removed with little exertion, but the type of ignorance that is the root of cyclic existence can only be removed with tremendous exertion. Indeed, the main topic of this series of lectures is how to bring about an end to ignorance. So far, I have been speaking about the presentation of the basis, the ground; with that as one's foundation, one practices. Today I will discuss to the levels of practice.

*Question:* What is the most skilful way of dealing with anger and aggression without either submitting to the aggressor or becoming angry and aggressive oneself?

*Answer:* If you let anger out and just keep expressing it, it is very difficult for this to be helpful. Since the technique itself promotes more anger, it will not bring about any positive result; it will only increase problems. Still, under certain circumstances it may be necessary to take counteraction to stop another's wrongdoing, but I believe that such measures can be enacted without anger. In fact, without anger, the implementation of countermeasures is much more effective than when your main mind is governed by a strong afflictive emotion, because under such influence you may not take the *appropriate* action. Anger destroys one of the best qualities of the human brain—judgment, the capacity to think, "This is wrong," and to investigate what the temporary and long-term consequences of an action will be. It is necessary to calculate such circumstances before taking action; free of anger, the power of judgment is better.

It is clear that if in a competitive society you are sincere and honest, in some circumstances people may take advantage of you. If you let someone do so, he or she will be engaging in an unsuitable action and accumulating bad karma that will harm the person in the future. Thus it is permissible, with an altruistic motivation, to take counter-action in order to help the other person from having to undergo the effects of this wrong action in the future. For instance, wise parents, without any anger, may sometimes scold or even punish their children. This is permissible, but if you really get angry and whack the child too much, then you yourself will feel regret in the future. However, with a good motivation of seeking to correct a child's bad behavior, it is possible to make a display, to make a show of an expression appropriate to what the child needs at that moment. Responses should be made in that way.

According to the Sūtra Vehicle, the usage of anger is not permitted in the spiritual path; however, within the Tantric system there is an explanation that it is possible to utilize anger in the path. In this case, the fundamental motivation must be compassion, but the temporary motivation is anger, and the purpose is to utilize the strength of anger without coming under its negative influence, so that practice becomes more effective. As in general life, actions of anger are swift, powerful, and effective.

*Question:* Is it better to leave hatred as a potential within oneself or to actualize it and thereby face it?

*Answer:* There is a practice in which in order to identify hatred—how the hated object appears, how one's mind reacts, what the nature of hatred is, and so forth—one allows the mind to generate hatred and then watches it, but this is not a case of displaying hatred externally and fighting with another person. If there is danger of your going outside with an angry attitude, it is better to lock your door—with yourself inside—and then generate anger and examine it!

For certain types of mental problems, such as depression[26] and some other mental crises, it can be helpful to let them out by talking about them; this reduces the uncomfortable inner feeling. For other kinds of mental crisis, such as anger or strong attachment, the more you express them the more they will occur; with these types, restraint will cause them to weaken. However, restraint does not just mean that when you develop anger or attachment to a high degree, you attempt at that moment to control it, for that is very difficult. Rather, in daily practice you should continuously reflect on the benefits and advantages of compassion, love, kindness, and so forth and reflect on the disadvantages—the faults—of anger. Such continuous thoughtful contemplation and development of appreciation of compassion and love, continuously revivifying such appreciation and increasing it, has the effect of creating dislike for hatred and respect for love. Through the force of this, even when you get angry, its expression changes in aspect and diminishes in force. This is the way to practice; as time passes, mental attitudes can gradually change.

*Question:* How is it possible for me to make effort in my meditation practice when there is no me, no I?

*Answer:* Most likely, this is the misunderstanding mentioned earlier, wrongly interpreting the emptiness of inherent existence as referring to an emptiness of existence itself such that it is viewed that nothing exists. This is wrong. If you think you do not exist, then stick a pin in your finger! Even if you cannot identify the I, that it exists is clear.

*Question:* I have received many teachings and initiations from my guru, but now I have lost some faith in him. What shall I do?

---

[26] For many ways of countering depression, see the index of *The Dalai Lama at Harvard.*

*Answer:* This is a sign of not having been careful at the beginning. If faith alone were sufficient, there would have been no reason for Buddha to have set forth the qualifications of a guru in great detail in explanations in the discipline, the sets of discourses, and secret mantra. It is said to be *very* important for both the guru, or lama, and the student to investigate each other. Still, this situation about which you are speaking does indeed occur; we should take such experiences as warnings and realize that we need a sounder basis—it is important to analyze, to investigate. I usually tell people that at the beginning, when receiving teaching, it is not necessary to regard the person as one's guru; rather, to simply consider the teacher to be a religious friend from whom you are taking teaching. Then if, as time passes, you examine the person's qualifications and gain real conviction, you can regard him or her as your own guru. This is a good procedure.

Now, to address your question about what to do: If the situation is that you first had faith and now faith cannot be generated, rather than coming to dislike the person, it would be better to develop a neutral attitude. In another way, it sometimes can be helpful to reflect on the fact that in Buddhism, and particularly in the Great Vehicle, even our enemy is one of the best gurus. Even though an enemy *deliberately* harms you, it is a basic practice to develop deep respect and a feeling of gratitude toward that person. If that is the case, then it is even more so here, since your guru is most likely not deliberately harming you. It can help your mental attitude to look on the situation this way.

*Question:* What are your opinions about Western students of Buddhism doing the practice of protector-deities?

*Answer:* This is a complicated matter. Whether one practices religion or not is in one's own hands, and what oneself does individually is one's own business. However, it is important to understand the context of such a practice. When we look into the past history of this tradition, we find that the theory of protector-deities comes from tantric practice. In the Sūtra Vehicle, aside from an occasional mention of the four great royal kings, there is no mention of deities other than the likes of Mañjushrī, Avalokiteshvara, Tārā, Maitreya, and Samantabhadra. In Maitreya's *Ornament for Clear Realization* at the point of the serial training in the six mindfulnesses, there is a practice of mindfulnesses of gods or deities, and indeed it might be possible that these latter deities as well as the great four kings appear within this practice. However, the context there is of being mindful of them as witnesses of your own actions.

On the other hand, *many* tantric texts mention protector-deities. In the Tantra Vehicle, a practitioner of a protector-deity first must gain initiation and then attain a deep state of meditation in which visualization practices of deity yoga eventually make one qualified to conduct this practice. Within imagining oneself as a deity in a mandala, one visualizes a protector-deity in front of oneself and gives him or her an order that has a use in a particular field of action. This being the actual process, if you want to engage in the practice of a protector-deity, first you yourself must be qualified.

In the past in Tibet, many people did the opposite, completely neglecting their own practice and simply running after protector-deities. This is absolutely wrong. One is supposed to achieve clear appearance of oneself as a divine figure within a full sense of being that deity, whereupon the protector comes under one's control; the practice is not at all a matter of the protector controlling oneself.

In fact, the best protector is Buddha, his doctrine, and the spiritual community. In a deeper sense, the actual protector and actual destroyer are your own karma. If you ask what really brings about help, it is your own virtuous actions. If you ask what really harms, it is your own non-virtuous actions. This is important. With what I have explained as a basis, you individually can make a decision on these matters.

*Question:* Must desire always lead to attachment?

*Answer:* In Tibetan there is a clear distinction between 'dod pa and 'dod chags; the first means desire, wishing, or wanting that can be either reasonable or not, whereas the second is necessarily an afflictive emotion. Reasoned desire exists even in the continuum of a Foe Destroyer,[27] someone who has gone beyond cyclic existence. Despite this verbal difference, at initial stages of practice when one is still a common being, it is difficult to distinguish between mere desire and afflicted desire, and one could even have

---

[27] *dgra bcom pa, arhan.* With respect to the translation of *arhan/arhant* (*dgra bcom pa*) as "Foe Destroyer", I do this to accord with the usual Tibetan translation of the term and to assist in capturing the flavor of oral and written traditions that frequently refer to this etymology. Arhats have overcome the foe, which is the afflictive emotions (*nyon mongs, kleśa*), the chief of which is ignorance, the conception (according to the Consequence School) that persons and phenomena are established by way of their own character.

The Indian and Tibetan translators were also aware of the etymology of *arhant* as "worthy one", as they translated the name of the "founder" of the Jaina system, Arhat, as *mchod 'od* "Worthy of Worship" (see Jam-ȳang-shay-b̄a's *Great Exposition of Tenets*, ka 62a.3). Also, they were aware of Chandrakīrti's gloss of the term as "Worthy One" in his *Clear Words*: "Because of being worthy of worship by the world of gods, humans, and demi-gods, they are called Arhats" (*sadevamānuṣāsurāl lokāt pūnārhatvād arhannityuchyate* [Poussin, 486.5], *lha dang mi dang lha ma yin du bcas pa'i 'jig rten gyis mchod par 'os pas dgra bcom pa zhes brjod la* [409.20, Tibetan Cultural Printing Press edition; also, P5260, vol. 98 75.2.2)]. Also, they were aware of Haribhadra's twofold etymology in his *Illumination of the Eight Thousand Stanza Perfection of Wisdom Sūtra*. In the context of the list of epithets qualifying the retinue of Buddha at the beginning of the sūtra (see Unrai Wogihara, ed., *Abhisamayālaṃkārālokā Prajñā-pāramitā-vyākhyā, The Work of Haribhadra* [Tokyo: The Toyo Bunko, 1932–5; reprint ed., Tokyo: Sankibo Buddhist Book Store, 1973], 8.18), Haribhadra says:

> They are called *arhant* [ = Worthy One, from root *arh* "to be worthy"] since they are worthy of worship, religious donations, and being assembled together in a group, etc. (W9.8–9: *sarva evātra pūjā-dakṣiṇā-gaṇa-parikarṣādy-ārhatayarhantaḥ*; P5189, 67.5.7: *'dir thams cad kyang mchod pa dang // yon dang tshogs su 'dub la sogs par 'os pas na dgra bcom pa'o*).

Also:

> They are called *arhant* [ = Foe Destroyer, *arihan*] because they have destroyed (*hata*) the foe (*ari*).
> (W10.18: *hatāritvād* **arhantaḥ**; P5189, 69.3.6. *dgra rnams bcom pas na dgra bcom pa'o*).

(My thanks to Gareth Sparham for the references to Haribhadra.) Thus, we are not dealing with an ignorant misconception of a term, but a considered preference in the face of alternative etymologies—"Foe Destroyer" requiring a not unusual *i* infix to make *arihan, ari* meaning enemy and *han* meaning to kill, and thus "Foe Destroyer". Unfortunately, one word in English cannot convey both this meaning and "Worthy of Worship"; thus, I have gone with what clearly has become the predominant meaning in Tibet. (For an excellent discussion of the two etymologies of Arhat in Buddhism and Jainism, see L.M. Joshi's "Facets of Jaina Religiousness in Comparative Light", L.D. Series 85, [Ahmedabad: L.D. Institute of Indology, May 1981], pp. 53–8.)

faith that is mixed with the conception of inherent existence, or compassion that is mixed with the conception of inherent existence, in which oneself and the object of faith, or of compassion, are wrongly thought to be established by way of their own character. It is difficult to distinguish between these at the beginning, but through sustaining basic practice one can gradually identify the factors of ignorance and the afflictive emotions, thereby making practice more and more pure.

## THE PATH

THE twelve links of the dependent-arising of a lifetime in cyclic existence are a presentation of our basic situation—afflictive emotions, contaminated actions, and suffering. Can the mind be separated from such ignorance or not? This needs to be examined. Any type of consciousness we might consider is connected with conditioning, with familiarization. Still, no matter how much a mistaken consciousness increases in strength due to habituation, since it does not have a valid foundation certified by correct cognition, it cannot be increased limitlessly. On the other hand, even though a consciousness that has a valid foundation might not now be very powerful due to one's not having become habituated to it to any great extent, by becoming conditioned to it the consciousness will—due to the force of gradually increasing familiarity—increase in strength. Moreover, since it is validly founded, it eventually can become limitless.

It is said that qualities that depend on the mind have a stable basis—the reason for this being that consciousness has no beginning and no end. Mental qualities have a constant basis, in that consciousness itself is their foundation, due to which, if one maintains practice, they do not require renewed exertion such as was involved in first acquiring them and hence their strength gradually can be increased. Once a mental quality is in the mind with a certain force, you do not again have to exert that degree of force to bring it to that level; hence, when you practice more, the additional training will increase that quality.

Since the root of suffering is ignorance, suffering stems from an untamed mind. Correspondingly, since relief from suffering stems from purifying and destroying the ignorance that is in the mind, it stems from taming the mind. Not taming the mind leads to suffering, whereas taming the mind leads to happiness. The taming of the mind is to be done mentally by training. Since the trainer is a particular type of mind, and that which is being trained is also the mind, one has to become skilled in psychology. Thus, in Buddhist texts a great deal of attention is devoted to the presentation of consciousness.

Among untamed minds, the most untamed type—the grossest level of mind that apprehends its objects erroneously—is called *wrong knowledge*. Then, as you become accustomed to the teaching and so forth, this is transformed into the level of *doubt*. Within doubt, there are three different levels; the lowest is doubt that is tending towards what is wrong, the middling is equal doubt that tends towards both what is wrong and what is right, and the highest level is doubt that tends towards what is right. Through practice, doubt is gradually transformed into a level called *correctly assuming consciousness*, which itself, through continued training such as by reflecting on reasons, turns into *inference*. By becoming accustomed to inferential understanding and by developing more and more clear appearance of the object being understood, *direct perception* realizing that object is gained.[28]

As a technique to overcome wrong knowledge that one-pointedly holds what is contrary to fact, you need to reflect on absurd consequences of your view, and thus Buddhist texts on logic present many forms of absurd consequences that break down the strength of adherence to wrong views. Then, at the point at which you rise to the level of doubt, it is possible to make use of syllogistic reasonings aimed at generating an inferential understanding. This is why it is important to study the books of the two pillars of logic, Dignāga and Dharmakīrti, in order to develop and increase the wisdom differentiating phenomena. In

---

[28] For more discussion of these seven types of awareness, see Lati Rinbochay and Elizabeth Napper, *Mind in Tibetan Buddhism* (London: Rider and Company, 1980; Ithaca: Snow Lion Publications, 1980).

the process, a practitioner gradually generates the wisdom arisen from hearing, the wisdom arisen from thinking, and finally the wisdom arisen from meditation.

## LEVELS OF PRACTICE

With this type of practice, you gradually come to see that indeed it is possible to transform consciousness. From this perspective, you can develop conviction in the efficacy of the practice of non-violence. The first level in the practice of non-violence is to restrain yourself from engaging in activities that harm others; the second is to implement antidotes to afflictive emotions that drive bad actions, and the third is to overcome even the predispositions that previously have been established by afflictive emotions. Through reflecting on how the unwanted faults of cyclic existence stem from ignorance, it can be concluded that you must practice these three levels of non-violence—first restraining the bad activities of the afflictive emotions, then restraining the afflictive emotions themselves, and finally restraining the predispositions established by afflictive emotions.

To remove latent predispositions, it is necessary first to extinguish the afflictive emotions, for without removing them there is no possibility of extricating the predispositions that they establish in the mind. The state of having entirely removed the afflictive emotions as well as their predispositions is called Buddhahood, whereas the mere removal of the afflictive emotions is the stage of an Arhan, a Foe Destroyer.

The destruction of the afflictive emotions and the predispositions established by them is like an offensive engagement; thus, prior to doing this, it is important to engage in a defensive line of action, making it such that you will not come under the influence of any of these counter-productive emotions. This is why it is important initially to restrain ill-deeds of body and speech. The final aim is the removal of all of the afflictive emotions together with their predispositions, that is, the attainment of Buddhahood, but in implementing the means for bringing about this aim, initially you have to make it so that you do not come under the influence of ill-deeds.

### Restraining the Bad Activities of the Afflictive Emotions

When you act with a selfish motive and commit wrong actions such as killing, stealing, adultery, lying, divisive talk, harsh speech, and senseless chatter, you not only harm others but also ultimately bring suffering on yourself. Thus, even not considering what violence does to others, if you consider the violence inflicted on yourself in terms of the cause and effect of actions and how you are led into cyclic existence, you can see that it is necessary to restrain ill-deeds of body and speech. By thinking along these lines, you will develop the conviction that harming others brings loss to yourself. This is to be reflected upon again and again.

It also is helpful to reflect on impermanence. No matter how long our life is, there is a limit to it, is there not? When we think about the formation of the universe and of geological time, the lifetime of a human is very short, and still there is no guarantee that we can live out even a certain lifespan of, say, a hundred years. Under these circumstances, it is senseless to concentrate all your energy, mental as well as physical, on accumulating money and property. Since it is very clear that wealth is helpful only for this life, it is appropriate to reduce extreme greed.

At this level of the teaching there is no reference to love and compassion for other people; rather, even if you consider only your own welfare, it is important to decide that these ill-deeds are not healthy. Also, if you think about the current world situation, it is clear that no matter how much material progress there is, it cannot fulfill what beings are seeking. Material progress alone does solve certain problems in some fields, but at the same time it develops new problems. Through our own experience we can realize that mere material progress is not sufficient.

Again, at this stage, it is helpful to reflect on the usefulness of our having gained the state of a human being. If you think about how the human body can be utilized in a positive way, you understand that it is really sad to use it for a harmful purpose.

Also, for some people it is helpful to reflect on the sufferings of the three bad levels of transmigration as hell-beings, hungry ghosts, and animals. If it is difficult immediately to believe that there are hell-beings, you can consider the many sufferings that animals undergo. With your own eyes you can see their manifold sufferings, but consider whether, if you were born in that sort of situation, you would be able to stand such suffering. We can, for the most part, decide that we already have many predispositions in our minds established by non-meritorious actions, motivated by beginningless ignorance, that will result in rebirth as animals. We have within our continuums causes just ready to develop into such lifetimes, and we need to consider how great the suffering will be if we are reborn into that type of suffering. Up to now, we have just looked *at* animals, but now we should imagine ourselves living with them *as* one of them; we should consider whether we could bear it or not. When we think in this way, we develop a sense of not wanting it. The "substances" that bring about these types of effects are acts of harmfulness and violence against others.

That is the first level of reflection on the faults of violence and the need to restrain from such activities—the need to restrain ill-deeds of body and speech. Still, there is no guarantee that even if you restrain ill-deeds of body and speech during this lifetime, you will not come under their influence in the next lifetime. Therefore, the best defense is to practice the next level of non-violence, which can be called an active engagement.

## Restraining the Afflictive Emotions Themselves

The afflictive emotions that bring about all this trouble for us are those mentioned in the twelve links of dependent-arising. Among them, their root is the ignorance that conceives objects as inherently existing; the force of this ignorance induces desire and hatred as well as many other types of afflictive emotion, such as pride, doubt, enmity, jealousy, and so forth. These are real trouble-makers. When we analyze the problems and crises of our present world, whether on the international level or in the family, it is clear that they are related to our anger, jealousy, and attachment.

Let us consider the so-called "enemy" who is hated with strong feeling. Due to the fact that this person's mind is untamed, he or she engages in activities to bring injury to us, and it is because of this that we consider the person to be an enemy. If this anger—the wish to harm—were in the very nature of the person, it could not be altered in any way, but it is not the case that hatred subsists in the nature of that person. Rather, just like ourselves, the person displays ill-behavior due to the influence of having generated an afflictive emotion. We ourselves engage in bad behavior, do we not? Still, we do not always think that we are completely bad. The situation is the same with this other person who is considered to be an enemy. Consequently, the actual trouble-maker is not the person but his or her afflictive emotion. The real enemy is an internal factor.

As practitioners, our real target or battle should be within ourselves. It will take time, but this is the only way to minimize counter-productive human qualities. Through such practice, we will attain more mental peace, not only in the distant future of another lifetime but day to day; definitely we will find more peace of mind, calmness—this is clear. The basic destroyer of our peace of mind is hatred, anger. Although all unhealthy attitudes are trouble-makers, hatred is the most powerful.

In order individually to create peace of mind, the question of whether the afflictive emotions can be overcome is crucial. At this point, one is training to overcome the afflictive emotions, and to do this it is necessary to destroy their root, which is the ignorance conceiving inherent existence. To do this, it is necessary to generate a reasoning consciousness that perceives objects in exactly the opposite way from how ignorance does. Only such a consciousness can serve as an antidote to afflictive emotions.

Since ignorance conceives phenomena to exist from their own side whereas in fact objects do not exist this way, to overcome this ignorance it is necessary to refute with reasoning its conceived object—inherent existence. We must realize that objects do not inherently exist or do not exist in and of themselves. It is crucial to ascertain through proper reasoning that the status of objects conceived by an ignorant consciousness actually does not exist. For this, reasoning must be used to refute the object that the erroneous consciousness apprehends. This is how a reasoning consciousness realizing emptiness comes to have great impact.

In order to develop the level of the view realizing emptiness required for serving as an antidote such that it can remove this ignorance from its root, it is not sufficient merely to generate an inferential consciousness realizing emptiness in dependence upon reasoning. In addition, one must bring this inferential under-standing to the level of direct non-conceptual perception of the truth of the emptiness of inherent existence, and in order to accomplish this, it is necessary to have the assistance of concen-tration. Through a deep level of concentration it is possible to develop a *samādhi,* or meditative stabilization, that is a union of calm abiding and special insight. This is the reason why it is said that in order to generate the wisdom-consciousness that is consti-tuted by special insight into emptiness it is necessary first to generate a calm abiding of the mind, a tranquilization and channeling of consciousness. Not only is it advantageous to develop the ability of the mind to remain on its object of observation in an alert and clear manner, but also when you develop vivid one-pointedness of mind, even if you do not believe in former and future lifetimes, your mind gradually, day by day, becomes more sharp, more alert, and more able. These are reasons behind the detailed presentations of how to achieve meditative stabilization.

Someone who wants to achieve mental calm abiding cannot live as we do now but should stay in an isolated place, where continual practice can be cultivated over a long period of time. In addition, if you work at achieving calm abiding in connection with tantric practices, it is said to be easier. Still, for those not capable or ready for such intense practice, it is helpful to rise early in the morning and immediately to use the mind—while it is still clear—to investigate what the nature or entity of mind is, without thinking about other topics. This practice helps to keep the mind alert, thereby helping throughout the rest of the day.

In order to reach the point where even internal subtle distractions have been pacified and your mind remains vividly and continuously on its object of observation, it is necessary first to restrain grosser levels of distraction, the coarse ill-deeds of body and speech that involve scattering of the mind to objects of desire and hatred. For this, you need the training in ethics. In the Buddhist system of ethics there are two levels—of householders and of those who have left the householder life. Even within the level of laypersons' ethics, there are several stages. The reason for there being so many variations is that Buddha set forth levels of practice in accordance with the varying capacities of individual people. It is crucial to follow a path according to your own mental disposition; only then will you gain satisfactory results.

Because sentient beings are of many and various dispositions and interests, Buddha set forth many different levels of practice. Recognizing this is helpful not only in gaining a proper perspective on Buddhist teachings but also in developing respect from the depths of the heart for the different types of religious systems that are present in this world, since they are all beneficial to those who believe in them. Even though the differences in philosophy are tremendous, often fundamental, still one can see that, relative to the interests and dispositions of various types of beings, those philosophies are appropriate and beneficial in the conduct of persons' lives. Through understanding this, deep respect will be engendered. Today we need this kind of mutual respect and understanding.

## Buddhism in the West

There are quite a number of Western monks and nuns in this audience. I respect your decision to take ordination, but there should be no rush to take vows. For, it needs to be remembered that since Buddha set forth practices in accordance with various different levels of capacity, it is critical to determine what your own level is and gradually to advance within that. It is important that those Westerners who sincerely want to practice Buddhism remain as good citizens and members of society—remaining in your own community without becoming isolated. It is important to adopt the *essence* of Buddha's teaching, recognizing that Buddhism as it is practiced by Tibetans is influenced by Tibetan culture and thus it would be a mistake to try to practice a Tibetanized form of Buddhism. By trying completely to Tibetanize your practice, in time there come to be difficulties, since such a system could not fit with your own mind and makes interaction with society difficult. Nowadays, some people are acting like Tibetans even to the point of keeping their heads down in an abject manner. Instead of copying such cultural forms, you should remain within your own cultural forms and implement Buddha's teaching if you find something useful and effective in it. Keep working in your profession as a member of your community. Although the various centers that are already established are useful and should be maintained, it is not necessary for someone who wants to practice Buddhism even to join a particular center.

Today we have discussed the first two levels of practice, of fighting against afflictive emotions. Tomorrow we will consider the third level, how to develop compassion in order to destroy the obstructions to omniscience, these being the predispositions established by afflictive emotions. Initially, one trains in ethics, which forms the basis of all later practice; then, through practice of meditative stabilization the mind becomes powerfully channeled such that it is effective in meditating on emptiness, whereby one eventually overcomes the obstructions to omniscience, which are constituted by the predispositions established by the conception of inherent existence. First, intellectually acquired obstructions are overcome, and then gradually the innate obstructions are removed. Within innate obstructions there are many levels of afflictive emotions to be overcome, but finally one completely extricates the ignorance that is the root of all afflictive emotions— the conception of inherent existence. This ignorance and all the afflictive emotions induced by it are extinguished, or pacified, in the sphere of reality. The wisdom realizing emptiness directly undermines the ignorance conceiving inherent existence, and the extinguishment of that ignorance in the sphere of reality is called liberation. As the protector Nāgārjuna says in his *Treatise on the Middle:*[29]

When actions and afflictive emotions cease,
    there is liberation.
They arise from false conceptions, these arise
From fictive elaborations.
Fictive elaborations cease in emptiness.

Contaminated actions and afflictive emotions are produced from wrong conceptuality, which itself is produced from the elaborations of the conception of inherent existence. Those conceptual elaborations are ceased *through* emptiness,[30] or, those elaborations are ceased in emptiness[31]—the final line being interpreted in both of these ways. With the instrumental, it means that conceptual elaborations are ceased *through* cultivating the view realizing emptiness, but also since that into which they are ceased or that into which they are extinguished is the reality of emptiness itself, it is also interpreted as that *into which* the fictive elaborations of the conception of inherent existence cease. That reality— the emptiness into which all of the afflictive emotions, ignorance and so forth, have been extinguished through the force of antidotal wisdom—is the true cessation that is liberation.

[29] *Fundamental Treatise on the Middle, Called "Wisdom"*, XVIII.5 (*dbu ma'i bstan bcos/ dbu ma rtsa ba'i tshig le'ur byas pa shes rab ces bya ba, madhyamakaśāstra/ prajñānāmamūlamadhyamakakārikā*), P5224, vol. 95. See the Bibliography for editions and translations.
[30] *stong pa nyid kyis.*
[31] *stong pa nyid du.*

# 4  The Value of Altruism

Wednesday Afternoon

## QUESTION AND ANSWER PERIOD

*Question:* I have heard that becoming drowsy during meditation on the breath may indicate that this particular method is not a suitable practice and that one should seek an alternative method. Could you please comment on this?

*Answer:* It often happens that when people meditate they become drowsy or even go to sleep; therefore, for some people with insomnia, I even advise them to recite mantra!

During meditation the mind can come under the influence of lethargy, a heaviness of mind and body, which leads to drowsiness and even sleep. Since this is due to the fact that the mode of apprehension of the mind has become too loose, a counteractive technique is to make the mind more taut, whereby it again is vitalized. If this does not work, then since states such as laxity and lethargy are caused by the mind's being withdrawn too much inside, one should imagine something bright or pay attention to the details of the object being meditated. If this does not work, one can leave the session and look far into the distance at a place where there is a vast view, or wash one's face, or go out into the fresh air.

If the particular person posing this question becomes unusually sleepy when concentrating on the breath but does not experience this when concentrating on some other object, the problem may be related to physical factors. In that case, it might be suitable to switch your object. It might help to meditate on a certain element or a certain type of light at a particular channel-center. Also, it might be advisable, while contemplating the breath, to meditate on light in the upper part of the body. In general, it is said that when the mind sinks and becomes lax, it is helpful to move the object upwards and that when the mind becomes excited, it helps to move the object downwards. The remedy has to be geared to the meditator's particular situation.

*Question:* What advice do you have for the parents of a seven-year-old child who has brain cancer? She is undergoing treatment in London at this moment.

*Answer:* No doubt the parents will use every means to bring about a cure medically. In addition, there are cases where it is helpful to employ meditative techniques such as repeating mantras and using certain visualizations, but whether these could be effective right away depends on a great many factors. In addition, in the Buddhist system, when one has tried whatever methods are possible and those have not been effective, it is most beneficial to reflect on the inevitable cause and effect of actions—*karma*. For those who believe in a Creator God they can think on such difficulties as being activities of God and gain help from this way of seeing things. The most important factor is that the small child must remain mentally peaceful. Beside these points, it is difficult to make suggestions. It is said that when the effect of an action is in the stage of manifest fruition, it is very difficult to reverse it.

*Question:* We are told that progress along the spiritual path depends upon faith. What is the substantial cause of faith?

*Answer:* In general, faith is of three types—the faith of clear delight, the faith of wishing to achieve a beneficial quality, and the faith of conviction. Concerning the main causes of faith, it is helpful to reflect on *reasons* that promote conviction and, beyond that, to develop actual *experience* yourself. As you think more and more upon reasonings, your ascertainment increases; this, in turn, induces experience, whereby faith becomes more firm.

Within faith and other types of spiritual experience, there are basically two types—one that comes by adventitious causes, suddenly sweeping over one, and another that comes by making hard effort over a long period of time. The latter is more stable, but adventitious experiences are indeed beneficial. It is helpful when you have a sudden, unusual, deep experience, to take hold of it and sustain it with effort right at that time.

*Question:* I find it difficult to comprehend all the different levels of practice. What is a simple basic practice that I could bear in mind?

*Answer:* In brief, it is what I usually say: At best, if you are able to do so, then help others, and if you are not able to do so, at least do not harm others. This is the main practice. The essence of the teaching of the Vehicle of Hearers is to refrain from harming others; the essence of the teaching of the Great Vehicle is altruism—the helping of others. In terms of the stages of practice, on the first level one restrains ill-deeds within the context of avoiding the ten non-virtues and then takes vows relative to that level; later one performs more altruistic practices and takes vows related with this vaster level.

*Question:* Is it possible to reconcile special love for one person, as in marriage, with equanimity? Or is it only possible to develop equanimity if one is completely non-attached with no personal involvements?

*Answer:* At initial stages of practice one has different levels of love—stronger for those who are, for the time being, closer to oneself and weaker for those who are not so close. However, as one practices and gradually develops, one's love becomes equal in strength toward each and every being. Such all-pervasive, equal love, however, cannot come right away; it must be developed gradually. As I was saying earlier, in the initial stages of practice love, compassion, faith, and so forth mostly are mixed at least with a little of the afflictive emotions.

*Question:* If a wholesome thought is followed by an unwholesome action, which has the greater karmic effect?

*Answer:* The effect depends upon the type of action done at the point of executing the action and also upon the extent of one's motivation prior to engaging in the action, how vast it is in terms of the field of motivation. There are cases in which the motivation, because of being powerful and vast, comes to be stronger in effect, and other cases in which the actual execution of the action comes to be stronger due to the situation—the object and the time.

*Question:* Many Buddhists find it disturbing to hear of Buddhist teachers who regularly break certain precepts by, for example, saying that it is permissible to drink alcohol, to cohabit with members of the spiritual community, and so forth. Are there ever any circumstances under which these precepts may be broken?

*Answer:* It is said in the scriptures of the Bodhisattva Vehicle that for the maturation of one's own mental continuum there is the practice of the six perfections—giving, ethics, patience, effort, concentration, and wisdom—and for the maturation of others' continuums there are the four means of gathering students—(1) giving material things to students, (2) speaking pleasantly by teaching about how to gain better lifetimes within cyclic existence and how eventually to leave cyclic existence, (3) causing students to adopt in practice what is helpful and to discard from within their behavior what is counter-productive, and (4) practicing oneself all of what one teaches others. Therefore, what one teaches others, one must also practice. With common sense we can understand that it is not suitable to explain practices to other people and then oneself do something else. Speaking frankly, when what a person teaches and what that person practices are contradictory, it means that he or she does not have the full qualifications of a spiritual guide.

It is said that it is important for a student—prior to making a religious connection with someone as a teacher—to understand the qualifications of a guru set forth in the Buddha's scriptures on discipline, in the discourses, and in Tantra and to analyze whether or not the person has these qualifications. Also, a person who wishes to become a lama teaching others must understand these qualifications and work at fulfilling them.

In the Mantra [or Tantra] system there is a mode of procedure for great adepts, who are at a very high level of realization, to behave in unusual ways. The boundary-line for engaging in these unusual activities is said to be when the adept has "attained capacity". What is the meaning of having attained capacity? The great Druk-ɓa Ḡa-gyu-ɓa scholar and adept, Padma Ḡar-ɓo,[32] said that this means that the yogi has attained an ability such that, through the power of yoga, he or she is capable of overcoming the non-faith that would be caused in others by the display of those activities. For instance, the great Paṇḍita Tilopā, despite displaying many unusual modes of behavior to Nāropā, was fully capable of overcoming any generation of non-faith. These unusual deeds may be done only after having attained such capacity. On the other hand, if in a situation in which a lama does not have such capacity he or she still tries to claim that these are the inconceivable, grand activities of a lama, this just indicates that his or her back is to the wall.

*Question:* Would you please explain the nature of the connection between an action completed many lifetimes ago and its karmic result as experienced through a natural disaster, such as being struck by lightning? Is it that our present consciousness, or mind-stream, affects or creates the lightning?

*Answer:* With respect to karma, it is relatively easy to understand through reasoned analysis that in general a virtuous action will lead to a pleasurable effect because of a mutuality of nature between cause and effect. However, when one considers a specific action at a specific time creating a specific effect at a specific time, these factors are extremely subtle and thus difficult to understand. With regard to the example of being hit by lightning, as I mentioned earlier, there are four procedures for researching or investigating objects, one of them being to examine the *nature* of an object that is not created by karma but is just naturally so, as in the case of heat and burning being the very nature of fire and as in the case of wetness and moistening being the very nature of water. Similarly, the production of lightning and so

---

[32] *pad ma dkar po*, 1527–92.

forth is through the machinations of the elements of this world system itself, but the fact that one was at the spot where the lightning hit—that one encountered this particular circumstance—is indeed due to karma. Many such distinctions have to be made.

*Question:* How can good Buddhists who are committed to not killing so comfortably enjoy the results of murder by eating meat, fowl, and fish?

*Answer:* This is a real point. In general, in Buddhism in the scriptures on discipline, the eating of meat is not prohibited. Also, monks and nuns are persons who, in a sense, are mendicants going out and begging for food and thus do not, when begging, state a preference, "I would like such and such kind of food." More than fifteen years back, I discussed this matter with a Shri Lankan monk, who said that, strictly speaking, Buddhist monks and nuns are, therefore, neither vegetarian nor non-vegetarian.

In the Bodhisattva Vehicle, the general emphasis is on being vegetarian; not eating meat is mostly considered to be preferable, and indeed some Japanese Buddhist communities are strictly vegetarian. I think that this is the proper practice. Then, in the Tantra Vehicle, the three lower Tantra sets—Action, Performance, and Yoga—prohibit meat-eating, but in Highest Yoga Tantra there is no prohibition against eating meat.

Those are general modes of explanation according to the scriptures on discipline, the Sūtra Vehicle, and the Mantra Vehicle. More specifically, it is unsuitable to have an animal killed for oneself. For example, in a market in a big city meat is already available to be bought and eaten, but in a place where no meat is available it is not suitable to say, "I want meat."

Still, the best way is to be vegetarian. I myself tried in 1965 to become a vegetarian, remaining so for twenty-two or twenty-three months. Then I contracted severe jaundice and was advised by my physician to discontinue vegetarianism. For those people who can follow strict vegetarianism, that is best. I was deeply impressed the other day when I heard on the BBC radio that the number of vegetarians in this country is growing. This is good news.

*Question:* You said that letting out anger was not a good practice. I assume you mean that it was not good to express anger to the person or object of the anger. However, some psychological systems advocate the expression of anger at a separate object, such as a pillow or a wall, as a release of the energy that resides in the angry person. Is this technique useful, or is it also harmful?

*Answer:* In principle it is not at all good to express or let out hatred. Nevertheless, if you neglect to implement an antidote, such as by cultivating patience and love, anger will increase. Thus, in principle it is better to try to minimize hatred. One of my friends says that when anger becomes fully developed, at that moment when he feels intense irritation, he hits himself. I also think that this could be helpful. The questioner mentioned hitting a wall or pillow; I think a pillow is much better, because it will not be so hard! Under particular circumstances it seems permissible to let anger come out, but without harm to others.

*Question:* Several of us had to tell a few lies at work in order to be able to come here and to benefit from your teaching. Is the bad karma acquired from telling lies countered by the good karma acquired through learning?

*Answer:* It depends on how much benefit is gained. If you implement the teachings in practice and thereby gain something for your way of life, then it is worthwhile. Whether it is beneficial depends on such factors. In Buddhism, as Shāntideva says, the most important considerations are the results of our actions; we have to distinguish what to do and what not to do in terms of determining what can be accomplished. With such a background, activities that are completely prohibited in the scriptures on discipline are not only allowed but are required under certain circumstances—they *must* be done if they will be beneficial. Just as, in medical treatment, different medicines are used even by the same person under new circumstances, so when furthering the process of purifying the mind, different circumstances or stages call for the implementation of different techniques. Let us return to our topic.

## THE BODHISATTVA'S ALTRUISTIC ATTITUDE

### Restraining the Predispositions Established by Afflictive Emotions

THE practice of the three trainings in ethics, meditative stabilization, and wisdom is capable of destroying the afflictive emotions; however, it is also necessary to get rid of the latent predispositions established by afflictive emotions, and this is extremely difficult. The reason for seeking to eradicate those predispositions is that they prevent simultaneous knowledge of all objects of knowledge. Even though persons who have achieved the state of a Foe Destroyer have extricated themselves from cyclic existence, they have not fully developed the potential of human consciousness—they are still only half-way on the path.

The question is *how* to destroy these predisposing tendencies. The actual weapon is the same—the wisdom understanding emptiness—but to overcome such latencies the powerful backing of great merit is needed. The technique for constantly accumulating great merit is unusual altruism. Until now, although the motivation of the person who is accumulating merit was aimed at liberation and not harming others, the main concern has been with this one being, oneself. In altruistic practice the concern is with *all* sentient beings.

Because sentient beings are limitless, when one's consciousness is concerned with this infinite number of sentient beings, the meritorious power that is accumulated by virtuous activities is limitless. For example, going for refuge to the Buddha, the doctrine, and the spiritual community out of concern for oneself and going for refuge out of concern for a limitless number of sentient beings are both instances of going for refuge, but they differ greatly in their meritorious power. This is because the former is concerned mainly with just one person whereas the latter is concerned with so many beings.

Also, until now, the aim has been to achieve mere liberation from cyclic existence—a mere extinguishment of suffering—for oneself; with the more altruistic motivation the aim is the highest possible attainment, Buddhahood. This is an extinction not just of the afflictive obstructions but also of their predispositions, which constitute the obstructions to omniscience. Thus, also from the viewpoint of the aim, or goal, the practices of the more altruistically motivated person seeking highest enlightenment will be more powerful in terms of accumulating a greater meritorious force.

The nature of an altruistic mind is precious, really marvellous. It is indeed amazing that the human mind can develop such an attitude, for one forgets oneself and considers every other being to be as dear as oneself. That is truly marvellous. If someone shows us warm feeling, how happy we feel, and it is the same when we show *other* people sincere concern. I think that with such an attitude, all of cyclic existence would be like nirvana. This is the real source of happiness, not only in the long run, but even today. If even the slightest experience of this develops, it will help by bestowing peace of mind and inner strength. It attracts the best of all experiences and provides the best ground for active participation in society. It serves not only as a teacher but also as the best friend and protector. It is truly good.

This morning we discussed the philosophical structure that allows us to draw the conclusion that it is possible to develop such a beautiful mind. Concerning the techniques for the development of altruism, the great Indian paṇḍitas set forth two ways—one through the seven quintessential instructions of cause and effect and the other through equalizing and switching self and other. The seven steps of the former technique are—after a preliminary practice of developing equanimity with respect to all beings—to (1) recognize all as friends, (2) reflect on their kindness, (3) develop an intention to repay that kindness, (4) generate love, (5) generate compassion, (6) develop the high resolve of universal responsibility, and (7) engender an altruistic intention to become enlightened.

About these, in order to generate such a strong altruistic

attitude in which you promise to seek Buddhahood for the sake of others, it is necessary beforehand to generate an unusual resolve in which you take on yourself the burden of others' welfare. In order to induce this unusual resolve, it is necessary to have compassion in which you cannot bear to see either the manifest suffering of others or that they are oppressed with unwanted internal conditions that will result in suffering; thus, from the depths of your heart you wish that they be freed from such a condition. For, without being stirred from the depths by compassion, the high resolve in which you take on the burden of freeing beings from suffering cannot be induced.

In addition, in the development of compassion it is clear from your own experience that it is easier to generate it for other persons who are attractive to yourself or with respect to whom you have a sense of pleasantness—who fit in with yourself—and thus you need a technique prior to generating great compassion to cause all sentient beings to appear appealingly, attractively suitable to yourself. This technique is to train in viewing all sentient beings the way you already view that being to whom you usually are the closest, whether this be your mother, your father, a relative, or another person.

Again, to view beings this way, it is necessary first to see beings in an even-minded way. It is helpful here to use the imagination. Imagine in front of yourself a friend whom you like, an enemy whom you do not like, and a neutral person. Examine your feelings to see which is being held closely and which is being considered in a distant manner. Naturally, you feel close to your friend; regarding your enemy, you feel not only distant but sometimes also anger or irritation; you just feel nothing for the neutral person. You have to investigate why these are so. The first one is my best friend; however, from the Buddhist viewpoint although today he/she is acting like a friend, it is not permanent, because over the course of beginningless rebirths, in some past lifetime he/she may have been one of my worst enemies. Similarly, although the other one is today acting like an enemy, I cannot at all be sure that in a past life he/she was not one of my dearest friends. In the future also, there is no reason why an enemy must always remain an enemy and a friend remain always a friend—there is no guarantee even within this life. Today's friend, within a short period of time, may show another attitude.

This is confirmed by our family experience and, even more so, in political life—today a good ally, the next moment the worst enemy! In this way, the basic life-structure is not at all stable: sometimes we are successful, sometimes unsuccessful; things are always changing, changing, changing. Therefore, that we experience such solid and stable feelings towards friends and enemies is absolutely wrong. There is no reason to assume such rigidity; it is foolish, is it not? Thinking in this way will gradually help your mind to become equal.

The next step is to think that, given that your enemy was in the past or will sooner or later be a good friend, it is much better to consider all three persons as the best of friends. Also, you can investigate whether there is value in showing hatred; what kind of result will come from it? The answer is obvious. However, if you try to develop compassion toward these persons, there is no question, no doubt, that the result will be nice. From this viewpoint also, you can see that it is much better to develop a compassionate attitude equally toward all three types of beings.

Extend this feeling toward your neighbors—one by one, to those living on this side and then to those on that side. Then, the whole country, then the European continent, then all of humanity in this world, and then farther to infinite sentient beings. This is how to practice the seven quintessential instructions of cause and effect.

The other technique for developing altruism is called equalizing and switching self and other. Here, you are to investigate which side is important, oneself or others. Choose. There is no other choice—only these two. Who is more important, you or others? Others are greater in number than you, who are just one; others are infinite. It is very clear that both do not want suffering and that both want happiness, and, in addition, both have every right to achieve happiness and to overcome suffering because both are sentient beings.

If we ask, "Why do I have the right to be happy?" the ultimate reason is, "I want happiness." There is no further reason. We have a natural and valid feeling of I, on the basis of which we want happiness. Merely this is the valid foundation of our right to strive for happiness. That is a human right, and it is a right of all sentient beings. Now, if one has such a right to overcome suffering, then other sentient beings naturally have the same right. In addition, all sentient beings are basically endowed with the same possibility to overcome suffering. The only difference is that oneself is single, whereas others are in the majority. Hence, the conclusion is clear; if even a small problem, a small suffering, happens to others, its range is infinite, whereas when something happens to oneself, it is limited to just one single person. When in this way we look at others as sentient beings too, oneself is not so important.

Let me describe how this is practiced in meditation. This is my own practice, and I frequently speak about it to others. Imagine that in front of you on one side is your old, selfish I and that on the other side is a group of poor, needy people. And you yourself are in the middle as a neutral person, a third party. Then, judge which is more important—whether you should join this selfish, self-centered, stupid person or these poor, needy, helpless people. If you have a human heart, naturally you will be drawn to the side of the needy beings.

This type of reflective contemplation will help in developing an altruistic attitude; you gradually will realize how bad selfish behavior is. You yourself, up to now, have been behaving this way, but now you realize how bad you were. Nobody wants to be a bad person; if someone says, "You are a bad person," we feel very angry. Why? The main reason is simply that we do not want to be a bad person. If we really do not want to be a bad person, then the means to avoid it is in our own hands. If we train in the behavior of a good person, we will become good. Nobody else has the right to put a person in the categories of good or bad; no one has that kind of power.

The ultimate source of peace in the family, the country, and the world is altruism—compassion and love. Contemplation of this fact also helps tremendously to develop altruism. Meditatively thinking about different reasons as much as you can engenders conviction, desire, and determination. When with such determination you try, try, try, day by day, month by month, year by year, you can improve yourself. With altruistic motivation every action accumulates good virtues—the limitless power of salutary merit.

## THE SIX PERFECTIONS

From a Buddhist viewpoint, what kind of help can we bring to others? One important type of charity is the giving of material things such as food, clothing, and shelter to others, but it is limited, for it does not bring complete satisfaction. Just as our own experience confirms that through gradual purification of our own mind more and more happiness develops, so it is the same for others; thus it is crucial that they understand what they should adopt in practice in order to achieve happiness. To facilitate their learning these topics we need to be fully capable of teaching them. Moreover, since sentient beings have limitlessly different predispositions, interests, dormant potentialities, and attitudes, if we do not develop the exalted activities of speech that accord exactly with what other beings need, we cannot fulfill all of their hopes. There is no way to accomplish this unless we overcome the obstructions preventing omniscience in our own mental continuums. Thus, out of seeking to help others we come to a decision to attain the stage of Buddhahood in which the obstructions to omniscience have been extinguished.

In this way, the Bodhisattva attitude is described as a mind that is aiming at the welfare of others as its special object of intent and is also aspiring towards one's own Buddhahood in order to accomplish this. Though your final aim is altruistic service upon the attainment of Buddhahood, in terms of actual present implementation you engage in the practice of the six perfections— giving, ethics, patience, effort, concentration, and wisdom—in accordance with your capacity, beginning with the charity of giving material things.

Charity means to train from the depths of the heart in an

attitude of generosity such that you are not seeking any reward or result for yourself. From the depths of your heart, the act of charity and all of its beneficial results are dedicated to other sentient beings.

Concerning ethics, the root practice of a Bodhisattva is to restrain self-centeredness. Since the practice of charity cannot involve any harm to others if it is to succeed, it is necessary to overcome from the very root any tendency to harm others. This must be done through eliminating self-centeredness, since a solely altruistic attitude leaves no room for harming others. Thus, the ethic of restraining self-centeredness is crucial.

In order to have pure ethics, it is necessary to cultivate patience. The practice of patience is extremely important since it is the main bulwark for training in the equalizing and switching of self and others. It is most helpful to practice in tandem the techniques that Shāntideva sets forth in the chapters on patience and on concentration in the *Guide to a Bodhisattva's Way of Life*,[33] the latter being where he explains the equalizing and switching of self and others. The practice of patience establishes the foundation, the basis, for equalizing and switching self and others. The reason for this is that it is hardest to generate a sense of affection and respect for enemies. When you think of enemies in terms of the practice of patience, not only is an enemy not someone who harms you, an enemy is the most benevolent of helpers. You come to think, "There would be no way I could cultivate the patience of not being concerned about harm to myself without someone to harm me."

As Shāntideva says, there are many beings to whom one can make charity, but there are very few beings with respect to whom one can practice patience, and what is more rare is more valuable. An enemy is really most kind. Through cultivating patience one's power of merit increases, and the practice of patience can only be done in dependence upon an enemy. For this reason, enemies are the main instigators of the increase of meritorious power. An

---

[33] *byang chub sems dpa'i spyod pa la 'jug pa, bodhicāryāvatāra.* See the Bibliography for editions and translations.

enemy is not someone who prevents the practice of religion but someone who helps practice.

In his *Guide to a Bodhisattva's Way of Life* Shāntideva states a hypothetical objection: "But an enemy does not have a motivation to help oneself and thus should not be respected." Shāntideva's answer is that for something to help it is not necessary that it have motivation. If motivation were necessary, there would be no way to have faith in the state of liberation from suffering. Thus even if enemies do not have a wish to help one, it is suitable to respect them since they are beneficial.

Then, a further complaint is lodged: "Even if the state of liberation does not have a wish to help, it also does not want to harm; an enemy, however, wants to harm." Shāntideva's answer is: "Because a person has a wish to harm, that person gets the name 'enemy', and you need an enemy in order to cultivate patience. Because a doctor, for instance, is seeking to help you, you do not identify him or her as an 'enemy' and hence cannot provide a situation for the cultivation of patience."

Such is the experience and reasoning of the great Bodhisattvas of ancient times. Thinking along these lines is very beneficial. Except for stubbornly holding on to self-cherishing, in time you will realize that cherishing others is something you must do—that there are many reasons why it is most fitting.

Another important type of patience is the forbearance that is the voluntary assumption of suffering. About this, Shāntideva reasons that if something can be done to fix a situation, there is no *need* to worry, whereas on the other hand, if there is nothing that can be done, there is no *use* in worrying.

Before suffering ensues, it is important to engage in techniques to avoid it, but once suffering has started, it should be taken not as a burden but as something that can assist. The reasons are many. Through undergoing small sufferings in this lifetime you can purify the karma of many ill-deeds accumulated in former lifetimes. Also, adopting such an attitude will help you see the faults and disadvantages of cyclic existence, and as much as you can do this, the more will you develop a dislike for engaging in non-virtues. It also helps you see the good qualities and advantages of liberation. In addition, through your own experience of suffering you will be able to infer what the pain of others is and to generate a wish to do something for them. Thus, when you think about suffering in this way, it can be seen that it provides a good opportunity for more practice and more thought.

The fourth of the six perfections is effort. One type of effort is like putting on armor; it prevents dissatisfaction with the lack of immediate achievement. Effort affords a willingness to engage in enthusiastic practice for eons and eons in order to bring about development.

The last two perfections are concentration and wisdom. I will talk about these next.

# 5  Compassion and Wisdom Combined

Thursday Morning

## QUESTION AND ANSWER PERIOD

*Question:* At the time of conception, does the consciousness mix with the developing physical aggregates, or can the consciousness join the physical body later, just a few moments before birth?

*Answer:* It is said that the consciousness enters at the time of conception itself. To murder a human means to kill either a human or something forming as a human, the latter referring to the period from right after conception until birth.

*Question:* Is abortion suitable when severe handicap has been medically detected in the embryo?

*Answer:* There might be situations in which, if the child will be so severely handicapped that it will undergo great suffering, abortion is permissible. In general, however, abortion is the taking of life and is not appropriate. The main factor is motivation.

*Question:* What are the karmic consequences of a woman choosing to have an abortion while understanding that it is wrong to take life?

*Answer:* It is said that if there are no mitigating circumstances, it is worse to do an ill-deed knowing that it is wrong.

*Question:* What advice can you give to those of us who have had an abortion but are currently practicing Buddhism?

*Answer:* When a faulty deed has already been done, then after learning that it was wrong, one can engage in disclosure of the faulty deed [in the presence of actual or imagined holy beings] and develop an intention not to do that action again in the future. This diminishes the force of the ill-deed.

*Question:* In the West there is a growing problem of drug and alcohol dependence. Do you have any advice as to how those afflicted can help themselves or be helped by those around them?

*Answer:* When drugs are taken, one's mind comes under the influence of additional delusion beyond that which we usually have. Double delusion is certainly not needed; what we require are techniques to relieve the basic situation. Knowing the nature of cyclic existence and training in altruism should help.

*Question:* Could you say something about euthanasia, which can be performed either by withholding treatment or by giving an active drug that kills the person in a few minutes.

*Answer:* Again, there may be exceptional situations, but in general it is better to let persons die at their own time. What we undergo is due to our own past actions, and we have to accept what our karma has impelled. Initially, we have to do whatever we can to avoid suffering, and then if nothing will relieve the problem, the suffering should be understood as the unavoidable result of former actions.

*Question:* Your Holiness, last time you talked about a subtle consciousness continuing as a stream from one lifetime to the next, but after liberation takes place, what happens to the stream of consciousness at the time of death? Does it continue?

*Answer:* The subtlest level of consciousness proceeds to and through Buddhahood. It is never extinguished.

*Question:* Many of us so enjoy living that we cannot imagine wanting to escape it; thus, some aspects of Buddhist philosophy seem unduly depressing. Could you please comment?

*Answer:* From a Buddhist perspective, this is a case of not understanding the various levels of suffering. If you are truly happy, then it is okay!

*Question:* To what extent does the lack of a concept of a Creator God prevent us as Buddhists from working and practicing alongside other religions?

*Answer:* Given the fact that sentient beings are of such different dispositions and interests, there are indeed beings for whom the theory of a Creator God is suitable and helpful, and thus you should not make trouble for yourself worrying about working alongside such a person. A considerable number of people who believe in a Creator God have reached a state without selfishness, and this proves that different teachings bring beneficial results. When we look at the results, respect for different religions grows.

*Question:* I have read about the Buddhist teaching of selflessness, which is often translated as "no soul". Yesterday you spoke about the subtlest continuum of consciousness as that which passes from one birth to another and is the inheritor of karma. Is there any essential difference between the subtle consciousness and the Christian concept of soul, leaving aside the question of reincarnation, which orthodox Christian teaching does not accept?

*Answer:* I wonder what a clear definition of soul is in Christianity. Since ancient times in India, there have been systems of tenets that assert a self, *ātman*, which is described as being permanent, unitary, and independent. This type of soul is not asserted in Buddhism.

*Question:* How can I overcome the strong fear of the unkind and hostile attitudes of others that I have experienced since childhood?

*Answer:* Cultivation of an attitude of cherishing others more than yourself will gradually help. It will take time. Also, if such a thought constantly causes discomfort for you, it would be better to try to stop thinking about it.

*Question:* What do you think of a Buddhist who does not believe in karma or rebirth?

*Answer:* This indeed needs to be considered. Generally, whether or not one is a Buddhist is determined by whether or not one asserts the three jewels—Buddha, his doctrine, and the spiritual community—as pure sources of refuge. However, there are persons who do this without much thought on complicated matters such as former and later births, karma, and so forth. On the other hand, some Western people who think more along these lines cannot immediately accept the three jewels and remain skeptical, but nevertheless have high regard for Buddha, his teaching, and the spiritual community. The latter, it might be said, are persons who are about to become Buddhists. Also, although Buddhists would not assert a permanent, unitary, independent self, there could be Buddhists who would not immediately accept selflessness.

*Question:* How is it possible to practice Buddhism while living among people—wife, husband, or family—who do not practice?

*Answer:* Buddhism is to be practiced individually; there is no necessity to recite texts together, for instance.

*Question:* What is your advice to an ordinary Westerner who is working but wants to complete Tibetan Buddhist practices without either becoming a monk or performing a three-year retreat?

*Answer:* Persons should remain in society carrying out their usual profession and, while contributing to society, internally carrying on analysis and practice. In daily life, you should go to the office, carry on your field of work, and return home. It would be worthwhile to sacrifice some late evening entertainment, go to sleep early, and get up early the next morning to perform analytical meditation. Then take a good breakfast and go slowly to your office or factory. Occasionally, when you have enough money, go to a Buddhist country for a few weeks. I think this may be practical and effective.

*Question:* How can we understand emptiness very simply without getting into too much intellectualized philosophy?

*Answer:* Is not what I have been talking about for the past few days rather simple? The main idea is that when objects are sought under analysis, they are not found, but this does not mean that they do not exist—it simply means that they lack inherent existence. If you contemplate this again and again, in time realization will definitely emerge.

*Question:* How do altruism and realization of emptiness unite in practice?

*Answer:* In the Sūtra Vehicle, the practices of the altruistic intention to become enlightened are the means for accumulating the collection of merit; it is under the influence of these practices that one meditates on emptiness. Similarly, meditation on emptiness accumulates the collection of wisdom. Then, within being influenced by the ascertainment that phenomena are empty of inherent existence, one cultivates the altruistic intention to become enlightened. I will discuss how these are combined in Tantra when I continue my talk.

*Question:* How should we help someone who is dying? What should we say to the dying person?

*Answer:* It is most important not to cause disturbance in the mind of a dying person, and also it is important to engage in a technique to activate memory of a virtuous religious practice with which the person is familiar. Those who do not accept the practice of any religion should be helped to die within a peaceful, relaxed attitude. The reason for this is that, as was explained earlier in relation to the twelve links of dependent-arising, the type of attitude that one has near the time of death is extremely important with regard to what karma is activated and thus how one will be reborn in the next lifetime.

For those who are engaged in Buddhist practice, there are many different levels of reflection that a dying person can put to use—reflecting on the meaning of emptiness, cultivating an altruistic intention to become enlightened, cultivating deity yoga, engaging in practice of the winds, and even reflecting on the exalted wisdom of undifferentiable bliss and emptiness, performing the transference of consciousness, and so forth. No matter how great the benefit or power of a meditation is in the abstract, it is crucial that the dying person be drawn to a practice that is appropriate due to previous familiarity. Since near the time of death the power of alertness and so forth deteriorate, there is no sense at all in trying to force a dying person to engage in an unfamiliar practice. It is most beneficial to remind the person of a practice that is appropriate to his or her own level.

## MANTRA

A s was mentioned earlier, within the context of an altruistic motivation the practices for maturing one's own continuum are the six perfections, and the practices for maturing others are the four ways of gathering students. Among the six perfections, each of the later ones is more difficult to achieve and is more important than the earlier ones. The last two perfections are concentration and wisdom.

In terms of the Sūtra Vehicle there are the thirty-seven harmonies of enlightenment for the sake of achieving liberation and many variations of paths for the sake of achieving Buddhahood, as presented in Maitreya's *Ornament for Clear Realization*. For all of these the root is the meditative stabilization that is a union of a calm abiding of the mind and special insight.

As a means of achieving in a quick and powerful way this meditative stabilization, there comes to be the Mantra, or Tantra, Vehicle, which comprises four Tantra sets—Action, Performance, Yoga, and Highest Yoga; the general mode of procedure of the three lower Tantras is roughly the same, although each has distinctive practices. In both the Perfection Vehicle and the Secret Mantra Vehicle the root of practice is the altruistic intention to become enlightened and the view of the emptiness of inherent existence, but the greatness of Secret Mantra comes by way of meditative stabilization. Thus it is even said that the scriptures of Secret Mantra are included in the sets of discourses,[34] since meditative stabilization is their main topic.

---

[34] *mdo sde, sūtrānta.*

In what way does the Secret Mantra Vehicle achieve its distinctiveness through meditative stabilization? How does it have a more profound way of enhancing the meditative stabilization that is a union of calm abiding and special insight? With the altruistic intention to become enlightened one is aiming at full enlightenment, the state of Buddhahood endowed with a Truth Body, which is the fulfillment of one's own welfare, and a Form Body, which is the fulfillment of others' welfare; from between these two, practitioners are specifically aiming more at achieving Form Bodies in order to be of assistance to others. Form Bodies have the major and minor marks of a Buddha's body, and in the Perfection Vehicle within the Sūtra system one seeks to achieve this type of body by way of accumulating meritorious power through practicing the six perfections under the influence of great compassion and the altruistic intention to become enlightened. The distinctive feature of Mantra is, in addition to these practices, to engage in a technique that is similar in aspect to the type of Form Body that is being sought—one meditates on oneself as presently having the physical body of a Buddha, this practice being called deity yoga. Since what one is practicing is concordant in aspect with the fruit one is trying to achieve, deity yoga is particularly effective and powerful.

In this way Secret Mantra has as a distinctive feature a yoga in which the entity of method and wisdom is indivisible. In the Perfection Vehicle, altruistic method and wisdom are separate entities that influence each other; altruistic method is affected by the force of wisdom, and wisdom is affected by the force of altruistic method. How does Mantra have an indivisibility of entity of altruistic method and wisdom? In the practice of deity yoga, within a single consciousness there are the two factors of imagination of a divine body and simultaneous ascertainment of its emptiness of inherent existence. Imagination of a divine body, which is in the class of compassionately vast appearances, accumulates the collection of merit, and hence a mind of deity yoga fulfills the feature of altruistic method. Also, since this very same mind ascertains the emptiness of inherent existence of the divine body and so forth, the collection of wisdom is accumulated; thus the same mind of deity yoga fulfills the qualities of wisdom. Although method and wisdom are still separable conceptually, they are contained in the entity of one consciousness.

A divine body in this context is one that a yogi intentionally imagines newly in meditation as an appearance—to that yogi's mental consciousness—of himself or herself in a divine body. Thus it seems that when yogis imagine themselves as being a deity and realize the emptiness of inherent existence of that divine body, there must be a difference in the impact of the consciousness due to this special object, which is the substratum of emptiness.

Also, when in the Perfection Vehicle one meditates on the emptiness of the self and the phenomena included in the five aggregates, one does not engage in techniques to cause the substratum—the emptiness of which is the object of meditation—to keep appearing and not to disappear. In the Mantra system, one specifically trains in keeping the appearance of the divine body in the midst of ascertaining its emptiness of inherent existence. Thus there has to be a difference from this point of view also. Since within imagining a divine body the mode of apprehension of the same consciousness ascertains the emptiness of inherent existence of that body, it is said that a factor of the wisdom-consciousness realizing emptiness appears as a deity.

## HIGHEST YOGA TANTRA

In Highest Yoga Tantra there is an even more profound way that the entity of altruistic method and wisdom is undifferentiable. This comes by way of focusing on more subtle physical and mental factors—the very subtle wind, or energy, and the very subtle mind, which themselves are an undifferentiable entity. To practice this level, it is necessary forcefully to stop the coarser levels of wind and mind, and many different techniques for doing this by putting concentrated emphasis on different places in the body are described in Highest Yoga Tantras. This is the practice of the channels, the winds, or internal energies, and the drops of essential fluid.

In general, the cultivation of special insight involves analytical meditation, but due to these special factors, in Highest Yoga Tantra it is stabilizing meditation that is emphasized when cultivating special insight. Coarser levels of consciousness induce ascertainment through analysis and investigation, but when one purposely manifests subtler levels of consciousness—not at times when these happen naturally due to the power of karma such as while dying but when they are induced through the power of yoga—these subtle consciousnesses in which the coarser levels have ceased are fully capable of ascertaining meanings. If one engages in analysis at that time, it causes the subtler level to cease and a coarser level to return. Since the subtler level of mind compensates for analysis—the purpose of which is to endow the mind with the capability of profound ascertainment—one does not analyze at that time, and stabilizing meditation is prescribed.

Concerning the mode of meditation in Highest Yoga Tantras, there are two main systems for achieving a Buddha body—through focusing on both very subtle wind and mind and through focusing only on very subtle mind. In most of the Highest Yoga Tantras of the New Translation Schools,[35] such as *Guhyasamāja*, *Chakrasamvara*, and so forth, the emphasis is put on both very subtle wind and mind in order to achieve a Buddha body. However, in the Kālachakra system[36] the emphasis is put only on very subtle mind, and in the practice of the Great Seal[37] and the Great Completeness[38] the emphasis also is mainly on very subtle mind.

From another perspective, it is said that, among Highest Yoga Tantras, one group focuses on the channels, winds, and drops of essential fluids in order to manifest the fundamental innate mind of clear light, and another manifests that mind through sustaining only a non-conceptual state without focusing on channels, winds,

---

35 Sa-gya, Ga-gyu, and Ge-luk.

36 For discussion of the Kālachakra system by the Dalai Lama, see Tenzin Gyatso and Jeffrey Hopkins, *The Kālachakra Tantra: Rite of Initiation for the Stage of Generation* (London: Wisdom Publications, 1985; second revd. edition, Boston 1989).

37 *mahāmudrā, phyag rgya chen po.*

38 *rdzogs chen.*

and drops. Within the first, there are Tantras that put particular emphasis on the wind-yoga, as is the case with *Guhyasamāja*, and Tantras that put particular emphasis on the four joys, as is the case with *Chakrasamvara*. The Great Seal and the Great Completeness are among those that manifest the fundamental innate mind of clear light through sustaining only a non-conceptual state.

Prior to engaging in the practice of Mantra it is necessary to receive initiation, and after receiving initiation it is important to keep the pledges and the vows that have been bestowed. In initiation, one person transmits a lineage of blessing to another, and even though blessings can be gained from reading books and so forth, there is a difference when a blessing is received from a living person's mental continuum in that its benefit forms more easily in the mind. Due to this, in Secret Mantra lamas are valued highly. We have already talked about the care one has to take with respect to accepting someone as a lama; here I will just add that it is said that when practitioners do not bear the proper form of the practice, it is an omen of the degeneration of the religion.

## TANTRIC DEITIES

Although Buddhism does not have a Creator God, in its many forms of initiation and so forth there are a great many gods. What are they? As was said earlier, from the beginning of Bodhisattva practice one is wishing for and aiming to achieve the altruistically active Form Bodies of a Buddha in order to bring vast, effective help to other sentient beings. In Buddhahood, Form Bodies appear spontaneously and without exertion in order to assist others. Just as when there is a reflection of the moon there has to be something to reflect it, so the spontaneous and exertion-less appearances of the Form Bodies of a Buddha need beings to whom they appear. Also, whether that reflection appears clearly or unclearly, big or small, and so forth depends upon that in which it is being reflected; similarly, the colors, shapes, and aspects of Form Bodies appear without exertion and spontaneously to trainees relative to their interests, dispositions, beliefs, needs, and so forth. In this way, the gods of the three lower Tantras appear in an aspect of making use of the five pleasurable attributes of the Desire Realm—pleasurable visible forms, sounds, odors, tastes, and tangible objects—but not in the context of partaking of the pleasurable attributes of the joining of male and female organs. For those trainees who cannot make use of these pleasurable attributes of the Desire Realm in the path, the Form Body of a Buddha appears as a supreme emanation body in the aspect of a monk, as did Shākyamuni Buddha.

To persons who have the disposition and capacity to practice Highest Yoga Tantra and whose capacities are activated, Form Bodies manifest in the aspect of male and female deities in union. Among them, to those who are capable of using the factor of hatred in the path, Form Bodies appear in a wrathful aspect, and to those who are capable mainly of using desire in the path, they appear in a peaceful aspect. Thus it is relative to trainees that Form Bodies appear in various ways.

A particular Buddha could appear as a single deity but could also manifest many emanations simultaneously. For instance, Guhyasamāja manifests as thirty-two deities in a mandala, but there are not thirty-two persons; there is only one actual person—the others are emanations. In this way, among the hosts of deities there are many that are just emanations, or reflections, of one being.

## THE VIEW IN THE FOUR ORDERS OF TIBETAN BUDDHISM

When the term "view"[39] is used, it is important to determine its meaning in context, since just as the word "feeling" can refer to both that which feels and that which is felt, so "view" can refer either to the consciousness that views or the object that is viewed. In Highest Yoga Tantra, the term "view" is predominantly used to refer to that which views, the consciousness that views. In its distinctive presentation, even though there is no difference in the

---

[39] *lta ba.*

emptiness that is viewed, there is a difference in the subject, the great bliss consciousness that views emptiness. Thus, from the perspective of the emptiness that is viewed Sa-ġya Paṇḍita (1182–1251) says that Sūtra and Mantra have the same view, and many Ge-luk-ɓa texts similarly speak about Sūtra and Mantra as having the same view, the reference being to the object that is viewed, emptiness.

Nevertheless, in Sa-ġya-ɓa four different views are posited with respect to the four initiations in Highest Yoga Tantra—the view of the vase initiation, the view of the secret initiation, the view of the knowledge-wisdom initiation, and the view of the word initiation. Similarly, Ge-luk-ɓa texts such as Jam-ȳang-shay-ɓa's[40] Great Exposition of Tenets[41] speak of Highest Yoga Mantra as being superior due to its view, the reference being to the subject that views—the wisdom of great bliss. Hence, when such scholars say that there is no difference in view between Sūtra and Mantra, they are speaking of the object being viewed, emptiness, since Sūtra and Mantra do not differ with regard to it. However, when they say that Sūtra and Mantra differ in view, they are speaking of the consciousness that views emptiness, since Highest Yoga Tantra presents subtler levels of mind that realize emptiness in a more powerful way. Ga-gyu-ɓa and Nying-ma-ɓa texts similarly say that the view of Mantra is superior to that of Sūtra; all of them are referring to a distinctive, more subtle type of mind.

Sa-ġya-ɓa texts present a view of the undifferentiability of cyclic existence and nirvana, saying that it is to be delineated in terms of the causal continuum that is the basis-of-all. There are slightly different explanations of the causal continuum that is the basis-of-all among the Indian paṇḍitas and within Sa-ġya-ɓa, but in a general way it refers to the real nature of the mind. From a different perspective, the Guhyasamāja Tantra speaks of different students of different levels of capacity, the supreme of which is called the "jewel-like person". The jewel-like person, himself or

---

[40] 'jam dbyangs bzhad pa'i rdo rje ngag dbang brtson grus; 1648–1721.

[41] grub mtha'i rnam bshad rang gzhan grub mtha' kun dang zab don mchog tu gsal ba kun bzang zhing gi nyi ma lung rigs rgya mtsho skye dgu'i re ba kun skong/ grub mtha' chen mo. See the Bibliography for editions and translations.

herself, could be described as the causal continuum that is the basis-of-all.

In Śa-ḡya-6a, the causal continuum that is the basis-of-all is identified by the great scholar Mang-tö-Iu-drup-gya-tso[42] as the fundamental innate mind of clear light. In another interpretation within Śa-ḡya-6a it is identified as all of the impure aggregates, constituents, and sense spheres of a person. It is also said that in the causal continuum that is the basis-of-all (1) all of the phenomena of cyclic existence are complete in terms of nature, (2) all of the phenomena of the path are complete in terms of qualities, and (3) all of the phenomena of Buddhahood are complete in terms of effects.

With respect to the equality of cyclic existence and nirvana, in the Sūtra system Nāgārjuna says in his *Sixty Stanzas of Reasoning*:[43]

> Both cyclic existence and nirvana
> Do not [inherently] exist.
> Just that which is knowledge of cyclic existence
> Is called "nirvana".

In the Sūtra system the reality—into which all true sufferings and sources of suffering are extinguished when one has thoroughly understood the meaning of the absence of inherent existence of cyclic existence—is nirvana. In a Śa-ḡya-6a presentation, the equality of cyclic existence and nirvana refers to viewing the impure phenomena of the mental and physical aggregates and so forth as primordially existing as pure mental and physical aggregates, and so forth. Four "mandalas" are presented as the foundation, these being the channels of the body, the winds, the drops of essential fluid, and letters; these are viewed as entities of the Four Bodies of a Buddha.

According to the thought of Mang-tö-Iu-drup-gya-tso, all of

---

[42] *mang thos klu sgrub rgya mtsho*; 1523–96.

[43] *rigs pa drug cu pa'i tshig le'ur byas pa, yuktiṣaṣṭikākārikā*; stanza 7. For the edited Tibetan with Sanskrit fragments and English translation, see Chr. Lindtner in *Nagarjuniana*, Indiske Studier 4 (Copenhagen: Akademisk Forlag, 1982), pp. 100–119.

the phenomena of cyclic existence and nirvana are to be viewed as the sport, or reflection, of the fundamental innate mind of clear light in that they are all of the same taste in the sphere of clear light. This is the view of the undifferentiability of cyclic existence and nirvana. Thus, the doctrine of the undifferentiability of cyclic existence and nirvana stems from the fundamental mind.

In Ga-gyu-ba, meditation on the Great Seal is done by way of four yogas—one-pointed, non-elaborative, one-taste, and non-meditative. The first two are said to be in common with the Sūtra path; through one-pointed yoga, calm abiding of the mind is achieved, and through non-elaborative yoga, special insight into emptiness is achieved. Through one-taste yoga, an extraordinary special insight is achieved in which all appearing and occurring phenomena are seen as of one taste in the sphere of the fundamental innate mind of clear light. When this path, which is unique to Mantra, increases in strength, it becomes non-meditative yoga. As Nāgārjuna says in his *Five Stages*,[44] which is concerned with the system of the *Guhyasamāja Tantra*, when one arrives at the level of the union of pure body and pure mind, there is nothing new to learn.

About the view of the Great Seal it is said:

The very mind is the innate Truth Body.
Appearances are the waves of the innate Truth Body.

The very mind, or basic mind, is the innate Truth Body—the fundamental mind of clear light. All pure and impure appearances are the sport of that Truth Body; they dawn from within the sphere of the fundamental mind of clear light.

In Ge-luk-ba, it would not be fitting to claim that a view like that of the Great Seal is the same as the view of the Middle Way, but it could be said to be a *special* view of the Middle Way. Within Ge-luk-ba such a special view is found in meditations on the view of the Middle Way that are mixed with Highest Yoga Mantra. When one thinks in these terms, the union of bliss and

---

[44] *rim pa lnga pa, pañcakrama*; P2667, vol. 61.

emptiness in Ge-luk-ba presentations of Highest Yoga Mantra and particularly the innate union of bliss and emptiness are the same as the Great Seal. Ge-luk-ba texts on Sūtra and even on Mantra put emphasis on the view as the object viewed, that is to say, emptiness; nevertheless, their texts on Mantra speak frequently about the view in terms of the subject, the viewing consciousness. Also, it is said that all pure and impure phenomena, within being the sport of emptiness, are also to be seen as the sport of the subject, the viewing consciousness, the innate mind of clear light. As Nāgārjuna says in his *Five Stages*:

> The yogi, while abiding in the illusion-like meditative
> stabilization,
> [Is to view] everything like that.

The yogi, while abiding in the illusion-like meditative stabilization, is to view all appearing and occurring phenomena—environments and beings within them—as the sport of the illusion-like meditative stabilization.

In the view of the Great Completeness, the mode of explanation is very different, but what it is getting at is exactly the same. As a source for this I mainly rely on the great scholar and remarkable yogi, Do-drup-chen Jik-may-den-bay-nyi-ma.[45] In the Great Completeness the root reference is to the fundamental innate mind of clear light, but it is called "ordinary consciousness".[46] A difference is made between mind[47] and basic mind,[48] the reference of "ordinary consciousness" being to basic mind.

In the Nying-ma-ba system, Highest Yoga Tantra itself is divided into three categories—Mahāyoga, Anuyoga, and Atiyoga. Atiyoga, or the Great Completeness, is also divided into three— the class of mind,[49] the class of the great vastness,[50] and the class of quintessential instructions.[51] As Do-drup-chen Jik-may-den-

---

[45] *rdo grub chen 'jigs med bstan pa'i nyi ma*; 1865–1926.
[46] *tha mal pa'i shes pa.*
[47] *sems.*
[48] *rig pa.*
[49] *sems sde.*
[50] *klong sde.*
[51] *man ngag gi sde.*

bay-nyi-ma says, all of the texts of Highest Yoga Tantra in all of the New Translation and Old Translation Schools teach just the practice of the fundamental innate mind of clear light. The difference between them is that, in the other systems, in the beginning stages of practice one makes use of many practices that involve conceptuality, through the route of which the fundamental innate mind of clear light is manifested, whereas, in the Great Completeness, right from the very beginning the utilization of conceptuality is not stressed and emphasis is put on basic mind in dependence upon quintessential instructions. This is why it is called a doctrine free from exertion.

Because in the Great Completeness there is tremendous emphasis on the fundamental innate mind of clear light, it has an uncommon presentation of the two truths, called the special two truths.[52] In a rough way, it could be said that what is fundamental and innate is the ultimate truth and, relative to it, anything that is adventitious is a conventional truth. From this perspective, the fundamental innate mind of clear light is empty of all conventional truths that are adventitious phenomena, and thus it is an "other-emptiness", that is to say, it is empty of what is other. Still, the fundamental innate mind of clear light is said to have a nature of essential purity and hence does not pass beyond the nature of the emptiness of inherent existence that is set forth in the middle wheel of Buddha's teaching.

Because this other-emptiness is set forth in a context of compatibility between the emptiness of inherent existence of the middle wheel and the Buddha nature as it is presented in the third wheel, it is said in some oral traditions that this is a "good" other-emptiness, whereas they call "bad" a teaching of an other-emptiness that stresses only the Buddha nature at the expense of the middle wheel, consequently advocating that the Buddha nature does inherently exist. In this way, many qualified scholars from all of the schools of Tibetan Buddhism—Ńying-ma-ba, Śa-ḡya-ba, Ḡa-gyu-ba, and Ge-luk-ba—have specifically refuted an other-emptiness that (1) presents a final truth that is itself inher-

---

[52] *lhag pa'i bden gnyis.*

ently existent and (2) looks down on the emptiness of inherent existence as an annihilatory self-emptiness to be derided.

As is said in an oral transmission from the great Lama Kyen-dzay Jam-ȳang-chö-ḡyi-Ī̄o-drö,[53] when the great Nying-ma-b̄a adept Long-chen-rap-jam[54] gives a presentation of the ground, path, and fruit, he does so mainly from the perspective of the enlightened state of a Buddha, whereas the S̄a-ḡya-b̄a presentation is mainly from the perspective of the spiritual experience of a yogi on the path, and the Ge-luk-b̄a presentation is mainly from the perspective of how phenomena appear to ordinary sentient beings. His statement appears to be worthy of considerable reflection; through it, many misunderstandings can be removed.[55]

## ACHIEVING A STATE OF SUPREME ALTRUISTIC EFFECTIVENESS

In the systems that put emphasis on both wind and mind, as an imprint of such practice, one achieves a union of pure body and pure mind—illusory body and mind of clear light—in dependence upon which the supremely altruistically-effective state of Buddhahood is attained. In the uncommon mode of procedure of the Mother Tantras, Buddhahood is achieved by way of a rainbow body. In the Kālachakra system, which emphasizes mainly the mind, Buddhahood is attained in dependence upon a union of a body of empty form and supreme immutable bliss. In the Nying-ma-b̄a system of the Great Completeness, which also emphasizes mainly the mind, in dependence upon bringing to completion four levels of appearance, all of the coarse factors of one's body are consumed and, much as in the system of achieving Buddhahood by way of the rainbow body, one achieves a rainbow body of great transference. All these are embodiments of wisdom and compassion that are for the sake of helping other beings extricate themselves from the round of suffering impelled by ignorance.

---

[53] *mkhyen brtse 'jam dbyangs chos kyi blo gros*, died 1960.

[54] *klong chen rab 'byams*, 1308–63.

[55] For more on how the four orders of Tibetan Buddhism come down to the same thought, see the final chapter in The Fourteenth Dalai Lama, His Holiness Tenzin Gyatso, *Kindness, Clarity, and Insight* (Ithaca: Snow Lion Publications, 1984).

# Glossary

| ENGLISH | SANSKRIT | TIBETAN |
|---|---|---|
| action | karma | las |
| affirming negative | paryudāsapratiṣedha | ma yin dgag |
| afflictive emotion/affliction | kleśa | nyon mongs |
| afflictive obstruction | kleśāvaraṇa | nyon sgrib/ nyon mongs pa'i sgrib pa |
| aggregate | skandha | phung po |
| aging and death | jarāmaraṇa | rga shi |
| attachment | tṛṣṇa | sred pa |
| birth | jāti | skye ba |
| Bodhisattva | bodhisattva | byang chub sems dpa' |
| compositional action | saṃskārakarma | 'du byed kyi las |
| compounded phenomenon | saṃskṛta | 'dus byas |
| conceptuality/ conceptual consciousness | vikalpa | rtog pa |
| consciousness | vijñāna | rnam shes |
| contact | sparśa | reg pa |
| conventional truth | saṃvṛtisatya | kun rdzob bden pa |
| conventionally | vyavahāratas | tha snyad du |
| correctly assuming consciousness | *manaḥparīkṣā | yid dpyod |
| cyclic existence | saṃsāra | 'khor ba |
| Desire Realm | kāmadhātu | 'dod khams |
| discipline | vinaya | 'dul ba |
| doctrine | dharma | chos |
| doubt | vicikitsā/ saṃśaya | the tshom |
| emptiness | śūnyatā | stong pa nyid |
| entity | vastu | ngo bo |

| ENGLISH | SANSKRIT | TIBETAN |
|---|---|---|
| entity/substantial entity | dravya | rdzas |
| exist validly | pramāṇasiddha | tshad mas grub pa |
| existence | bhava | srid pa |
| existent | sat | yod pa |
| existing by way of its own character | svalakṣaṇasiddha | rang gi mtshan nyid kyis grub pa |
| existing in its own right | svarūpasiddha | rang ngos nas grub pa |
| existing inherently | svabhāvasiddha | rang bzhin gyis grub pa |
| external object | bāhyārtha | phyi don |
| feeling | vedanā | tshor ba |
| Foe Destroyer | arhan | dgra bcom pa |
| form | rūpa | gzugs |
| Form Body | rūpakāya | gzugs sku |
| Form Realm | rūpadhātu | gzugs khams |
| Formless Realm | ārūpyadhātu | gzugs med khams |
| fruit | phala | 'bras bu |
| grasping | upādāna | len pa |
| Hearer | śrāvaka | nyan thos |
| highest enlightenment | anuttarasambuddha | bla na med pa'i byang chub |
| ignorance | avidyā | ma rig pa |
| impermanent | anitya | mi rtag pa |
| imputedly existent | prajñaptisat | btags yod |
| inferential valid cognition | anumānapramāṇa | rjes su dpag pa'i tshad ma |
| inherently existent | svabhāvasiddha | rang bzhin gyis grub pa |
| Jewel/Superior Rarity | ratna | dkon mchog |
| latency/predisposition | vāsanā | bag chags |
| Manifest Knowledge | abhidharma | chos mngon pa |
| meditative stabilization | samādhi | ting nge 'dzin |
| mental and physical aggregates | skandha | phung po |
| mental consciousness | manovijñāna | yid kyi rnam shes |
| mental factor | caitta | sems byung |
| mind | citta | sems |
| mind generation of altruistic aspiration to highest enlightenment | bodhicittaparamotpāda | byang chub mchog tu sems bskyed pa |
| mind-basis-of-all | ālayavijñāna | kun gzhi rnam par shes pa |
| mistaken consciousness | bhrāntijñāna | 'khrul shes |

| ENGLISH | SANSKRIT | TIBETAN |
|---|---|---|
| name and form | nāmarūpa | ming gzugs |
| negative phenomenon | pratiṣedha | dgag pa |
| non-affirming negative | prasajyapratiṣedha | med dgag |
| | | |
| object | viṣaya | yul |
| object of knowledge | jñeya | shes bya |
| obstruction to liberation/ | kleśāvaraṇa | nyon sgrib |
| afflictive obstruction | | |
| obstruction to omniscience/ | jñeyāvaraṇa | shes sgrib |
| obstruction to | | |
| simultaneous cognition | | |
| of all phenomena | | |
| | | |
| path | mārga | lam |
| path of accumulation | saṃbhāramārga | tshogs lam |
| path of meditation | bhāvanāmārga | sgom lam |
| path of no more learning | aśaikṣamārga | mi slob lam |
| path of preparation | prayogamārga | sbyor lam |
| path of seeing | darśanamārga | mthong lam |
| person | puruṣa | skyes bu |
| person's emptiness of being | nityaikasvatantra- | gang zag rtag gcig rang |
| permanent, unitary, and | śūnyapudgala | dbang can gyis stong pa |
| independent | | |
| product | kṛta | byas pa |
| | | |
| reason | hetu | gtan tshigs |
| | | |
| self | ātman | bdag |
| selflessness of persons | pudgalanairātmya | gang zag gi bdag med |
| selflessness of phenomena | dharmanairātmya | chos kyi bdag med |
| sentient being | sattva | sems can |
| sets of discourses | sūtrānta | mdo sde |
| six sense spheres | ṣaḍāyatana | skye mched drug |
| Solitary Realizer | pratyekabuddha | rang sangs rgyas |
| space | ākāśa | nam mkha' |
| special insight | vipaśyanā | lhag mthong |
| Spiritual Community | saṅgha | dge 'dun |
| substantially established | dravyasiddha | rdzas grub |
| substantially existent | dravyasat | rdzas yod |
| Sūtra | sūtra | mdo |
| | | |
| tangible object | spraṣṭavya | reg bya |
| thing/functioning thing | bhāva | dngos po |
| truly established/truly | satyasiddha | bden par grub pa |
| existent | | |

| ENGLISH | SANSKRIT | TIBETAN |
|---------|----------|---------|
| truly existent/truly established | satyasat | bden par yod pa |
| truth | satya | bden pa |
| Truth Body | dharmakāya | chos sku |
| | | |
| ultimate truth | paramārthasatya | don dam bden pa |
| ultimately | paramārthatas | don dam par |
| uncompounded [phenomenon] | asaṃskṛta | 'dus ma byas |
| | | |
| valid cognition | pramāṇa | tshad ma |
| | | |
| wrong consciousness | viparyayajña | log shes |

# Bibliography

Indian and Tibetan treatises are listed alphabetically by author in the second section. Other works are listed alphabetically by author in the third section. 'P', standing for 'Peking edition', refers to the *Tibetan Tripiṭaka* (Tokyo-Kyoto: Tibetan Tripiṭaka Research Foundation, 1956).

## SŪTRA

*Rice Seedling Sūtra*
śālistambasūtra
sā lu'i ljang pa'i mdo
P876, vol. 34
    Sanskrit and Tibetan texts: *Śālistamba Sūtra, Pratītya-Samutpāda-vibhaṅga Nirde-śasūtra, and Pratītyasamutpādagāthā Sūtra.* N. Aiyaswami Sastri, ed. Adyar, Madras: Vasanta Press, The Theosophical Society, 1950

## SANSKRIT AND TIBETAN WORKS

Chandrakīrti (zla ba grags pa, seventh century)
    *Clear Words, Commentary on (Nāgārjuna's) "Treatise on the Middle"*
    mūlamadhyamakavṛttiprasannapadā
    dbu ma rtsa ba'i 'grel pa tshig gsal ba
    P5260, vol. 98
    Also: Dharamsala: Tibetan Publishing House, 1968
    Sanskrit: *Mūlamadhyamakakārikās de Nāgārjuna avec la Prasannapadā Commentaire de Candrakīrti.* Louis de la Vallée Poussin, ed. Bibliotheca Buddhica IV. Osnabrück: Biblio Verlag, 1970
    English translation (Ch.I, XXV): T. Stcherbatsky. *Conception of Buddhist Nirvāṇa.* Leningrad: Office of the Academy of Sciences of the USSR, 1927; revised rpt. Delhi: Motilal Banarsidass, 1978, pp. 77–222
    English translation (Ch.II): Jeffrey Hopkins. "Analysis of Coming and Going". Dharamsala: Library of Tibetan Works and Archives, 1974
    Partial English translation: Mervyn Sprung. *Lucid Exposition of the Middle Way, the*

*Essential Chapters from the Prasannapadā of Candrakīrti translated from the Sanskrit.* London: Routledge, 1979 and Boulder: Prajñā Press, 1979
French translation (Ch.II-IV, VI-IX, XI, XXIII, XXIV, XXVI, XXVII): Jacques May. *Prasannapadā Madhyamaka-vṛtti, douze chapitres traduits du sanscrit et du tibé-tain.* Paris: Adrien-Maisonneuve, 1959
French translation (Ch.XVIII-XXII): J.W. de Jong. *Cinq chapitres de la Prasanna-padā.* Paris: Geuthner, 1949
French translation (Ch.XVII): É. Lamotte. "Le Traitéde l'acte de Vasubandhu, Karmasiddhiprakaraṇa", *Mélanges Chinois et Bouddhiques* 4 (1936), 265–288
German translation (Ch.V and XII-XVI): St. Schayer. Ausgewhälte Kapitel aus der Prasannapadā. Krakow: Naktadem Polskiej Akademji Umiejetnosci, 1931
German translation (Ch.X): St. Schayer. "Feuer und Brennstoff". *Rocznik Orjental-istyczny* 7 (1931), pp. 26–52


Jam-ȳang-shay-b̄a (*'jam dbyangs bzhad pa,* 1648–1721)
*Great Exposition of Tenets: Explanation of 'Tenets', Sun of the Land of Samantabhadra Brilliantly Illuminating All of Our Own and Others' Tenets and the Meaning of the Profound [Emptiness], Ocean of Scripture and Reasoning Fulfilling All Hopes of All Beings*
grub mtha' chen mo/ grub mtha'i rnam bshad rang gzhan grub mtha' kun dang zab don mchog tu gsal ba kun bzang zhing gi nyi ma lung rigs rgya mtsho skye dgu'i re ba kun skong
Musoorie: Dalama, 1962
English translation (beginning of the chapter on the Consequence School): Jeffrey Hopkins. In *Meditation on Emptiness.* London: Wisdom Publications, 1983


Nāgārjuna (*klu sgrub,* first to second century C.E.)
*Treatise on the Middle/ Fundamental Treatise on the Middle, Called "Wisdom"*
madhyamakaśāstra/prajñānāmamūlamadhyamakakārikā
dbu ma'i bstan bcos/ dbu ma rtsa ba'i tshig le'ur byas pa shes rab ces bya ba
P5224, vol. 95
Edited Sanskrit: *Nāgārjuna, Mūlamadhyamakakārikāḥ.* J.W. de Jong, ed. Adyar: Adyar Library and Research Centre, 1977. Also: Chr. Lindtner in *Nāgārjuna's Filosofiske Vaerker.* Indiske Studier 2, pp. 177–215. Copenhagen: Akademisk Forlag, 1982
English translation: Frederick Streng. Emptiness: *A Study in Religious Meaning.* Nashville, New York: Abingdon Press, 1967. Also: Kenneth Inada. *Nāgārjuna: A Translation of his Mūlamadhyamakakārikā.* Tokyo, The Hokuseido Press, 1970. Also: David J. Kalupahana. *Nāgārjuna: The Philosophy of the Middle Way.* Albany: State University Press of New York, 1986
Italian translation: R. Gnoli. *Nāgārjuna: Madhyamaka Kārikā, Le stanze del cammino di mezzo.* Enciclopedia di autori classici 61. Turin: P. Boringhieri, 1961
Danish translation: Chr. Lindtner in *Nāgārjuna's Filosofiske Vaerker.* Indiske Studier 2, pp. 67–135. Copenhagen: Akademisk Forlag, 1982
*Seventy Stanzas on Emptiness*
śūnyatāsaptatikārikā

stong pa nyid bdun cu pa'i tshig le'ur byas pa
P5227, vol.95; Toh 3827, Tokyo *sde dge* vol.1
Edited Tibetan and English translation: Chr. Lindtner in *Nagarjuniana*. Indiske
Studier 4, pp.34–69. Copenhagen: Akademisk Forlag, 1982
English translation: David Ross Komito. *Nāgārjuna's "Seventy Stanzas": A Buddhist Psychology of Emptiness*. Ithaca: Snow Lion Publications, 1987
**Sixty Stanzas of Reasoning**
yuktiṣaṣṭikākārikā
rigs pa drug cu pa'i tshig le'ur byas pa
P5225, vol. 95; Toh 3825, Tokyo *sde dge* vol. 1
Edited Tibetan with Sanskrit fragments and English translation: Chr. Lindtner in
*Nagarjuniana*. Indiske Studier 4, pp. 100–119. Copenhagen: Akademisk Forlag,
1982


Shāntideva (*zhi ba lha*, eighth century)
*A Guide to the Bodhisattva's Way of Life/Engaging in the Bodhisattva Deeds*
bodhi[sattva]caryāvatāra
byang chub sems dpa'i spyod pa la 'jug pa
P5272, vol. 99
Sanskrit and Tibetan texts: Vidhushekara Bhattacharya, ed. *Bodhicaryāvatāra*.
Bibliotheca Indica, vol. 280. Calcutta: The Asiatic Society, 1960
English translation: Stephen Batchelor. *A Guide to the Bodhisattva's Way of Life*.
Dharamsala: Library of Tibetan Works and Archives, 1979. Also: Marion
Matics. *Entering the Path of Enlightenment*. New York: Macmillan Co., 1970
Contemporary commentary by Geshe Kelsang Gyatso. *Meaningful to Behold*.
*London*: Wisdom Publications, 1980


Vasubandhu (*dbyig gnyen*, fl.360)
*Treasury of Knowledge*
abhidharmakośakārikā
chos mngon pa'i mdzod kyi tshig le'ur byas pa
P5590, vol. 115
Sanskrit text: P. Pradhan, ed. *Abhidharmakośabhāṣyam of Vasubandhu*. Patna:
Jayaswal Research Institute, 1975
French translation: Louis de la Vallée Poussin. *L'Abhidharmakośa de Vasubandhu*.
6 vols. Bruxelles: Institut Belge des Hautes Études Chinoises, 1971
English translation from the French: Leo M. Pruden, *Abhidharmakośabhāṣyam*. 4
vols. Freemont, CA.: Asian Humanities Press, 1988–89.


OTHER WORKS

Dalai Lama, Benson, Thurman, Goleman, et al. *Mind Science: An East-West Dialogue*.
Boston: Wisdom Publications, 1991.

Gyatso, Tenzin, Dalai Lama XIV. *The Dalai Lama at Harvard: Lectures on the Buddhist
Path to Peace*. Ithaca: Snow Lion Publications, 1989. Jeffrey Hopkins, trans. and ed.

Gyatso, Tenzin, Dalai Lama XIV and Jeffrey Hopkins. *The Kālachakra Tantra: Rite of Initiation for the Stage of Generation.* London: Wisdom Publications, 1985.

Gyatso, Tenzin, Dalai Lama XIV. *Kindness, Clarity, and Insight.* Jeffrey Hopkins, trans. and ed.; Elizabeth Napper, co-editor. Ithaca.: Snow Lion Publications, 1984.

Hopkins, Jeffrey. *Meditation on Emptiness.* London: Wisdom Publications, 1983.

Joshi, L.M. "Facets of Jaina Religiousness in Comparative Light", L.D. Series 85. Ahmedabad: L.D. Institute of Indology, May 1981. pp. 53-8

Lati Rinbochay and Elizabeth Napper. *Mind in Tibetan Buddhism.* London: Rider, 1980; rpt. Ithaca: Snow Lion Publications, 1980.

Lati Rinbochay and Jeffrey Hopkins. *Death, Intermediate State, and Rebirth in Tibetan Buddhism.* London: Rider, 1979; Ithaca: Snow Lion Publications, 1980.

Lindtner, Christian. *Nagarjuniana.* Indiske Studier 4. Copenhagen: Akademisk Forlag, 1982.

Poussin, Louis de la Vallée. *L'Abhidharmakośa de Vasubandhu.* 6 vols. Bruxelles: Institut Belge des Hautes Études Chinoises, 1971.

Tharchin, Sermey Geshe Lobsang. *King Udrayana and the Wheel of Life.* Howell, New Jersey: Mahayana Sutra and Tantra Press, 1984.

Wogihara, Unrai, ed. *Abhisamayālaṃkārālokā Prajñā-pāramitā-vyākhyā. The Work of Haribhadra.* Tokyo: The Toyo Bunko, 1932–5; rpt. ed., Tokyo: Sankibo Buddhist Book Store, 1973.

# Index

# The Author

THE DALAI LAMA OF TIBET is internationally recognized as a spokesman for peace, non-violence and understanding among different cultures and religions. He has resided in exile in India since 1959, when China forcefully occupied Tibet. He leads the Tibetan government in exile in Dharamsala, India, and has worked to establish educational, cultural and religious institutions to preserve the Tibetan culture. In 1989, he received the Nobel Peace Prize. The official announcement of the award was as follows:

*"The Norwegian Nobel Committee has decided to award the 1989 Nobel Peace Prize to the Fourteenth Dalai Lama, Tenzin Gyatso, the religious and political leader of the Tibetan people.*

*The Committee wants to emphasize the fact that the Dalai Lama in his struggle for the liberation of Tibet consistently has opposed the use of violence. He has instead advocated peaceful solutions based upon tolerance and mutual respect in order to preserve the historical and cultural heritage of his people.*

*The Dalai Lama has developed his philosophy of peace from a great reverence for all things living and upon the concept of universal responsibility embracing all mankind as well as nature.*

*In the opinion of the Committee the Dalai Lama has come forward with constructive and forward-looking proposals for the solution of international conflicts, human rights issues, and global environmental problems."*

# The Translator

JEFFREY HOPKINS is Professor of Religious Studies at the University of Virginia, where he teaches Indo-Tibetan Buddhist Studies and Tibetan language. He received a B.A from Harvard University in 1963, trained for five years at the Tibetan Buddhist Learning Center in New Jersey, and received a Ph.D. in Buddhist Studies from the University of Wisconsin in 1973. He has published over a dozen articles and eighteen books, the most prominent of which is *Meditation on Emptiness*. At the University of Virginia he is Director of the Center for South Asian Studies and has founded programs in Buddhist Studies and Tibetan language. From 1979 to 1989 he served as the Dalai Lama's chief interpreter on lecture tours in the US, Canada, Southeast Asia, Great Britain, and Switzerland; eight of his books are collaborations with the Dalai Lama. He is currently writing an analysis of Tibetan interpretations of the Mind Only doctrine of emptiness.

# Wisdom Publications

WISDOM PUBLICATIONS is a non-profit publisher of books on Buddhism, Tibet and related East-West themes. Our titles are published in appreciation of Buddhism as a living philosophy and with the special commitment to preserve and transmit important works from all the major Buddhist traditions. Wisdom is also the largest Buddhist book distributor in the world with over 3,000 titles from over 100 publishers worldwide. We stock a wide range of titles by the Dalai Lama and other eminent Buddhist teachers.

For more information, or a copy of our extensive mail order catalogue, please write to us at 361 Newbury Street, Boston, Massachusetts, 02115, USA.

Wisdom is a non-profit, charitable 501(c)(3) organization and a part of the Foundation for the Preservation of the Mahayana Tradition (FPMT).